Maimonides on the "Decline of the Generations"
and the Nature of Rabbinic Authority

SUNY Series in Jewish Philosophy
Kenneth Seeskin, Editor

Maimonides
on
the "Decline of the Generations"
and
the Nature of Rabbinic Authority

Menachem Kellner

State University of New York Press

Published by
State University of New York Press, Albany

For information, address State University of New York
Press, State University Plaza, Albany, N.Y., 12246

Production by Diane Ganeles
Marketing by Fran Keneston

Library of Congress Cataloging-in-Publication Data

Kellner, Menachem Marc, 1946-
    Maimonides on the "Decline of the generations" and the nature of
rabbinic authority / Menachem Kellner.
        p.   cm.—(SUNY series in Jewish philosophy)
    Includes bibliographical references and index.
    ISBN 0-7914-2922-9 (pb acid-free). —ISBN 0-7914-2921-0 (ch acid
    -free)
    1. Maimonides, Moses, 1135-1204—Views on Jewish tradition.
    2. Tradition (Judaism)   3. Jewish law—Interpretation and
    construction.   4. Judaism and science.   5. Judaism and philosophy.
    I. Title.   II. Series.
    BM529.K45   1996
    296.6'1—dc20   95-19975
                                                                    CIP

10 9 8 7 6 5 4 3 2 1

To the Memory
of
Rabbi Abraham B. Shoulson

Loving Grandfather to my Children

Contents

Preface

The "quarrel of the ancients and moderns" is a well-known trope in
Western cultural history. In various generations, "moderns" have sought to
assert equality with or superiority over the classical world. Whenever such
assertions were put forward, defenders of the classics would arise to defend
the superiority of the "ancients" over the "moderns."[1]

The premodern Jewish world knew no such quarrel: the superiority of
the ancients over the moderns was taken as being so clear and so basic that
it was rarely even clearly asserted and almost never explicitly and self-
consciously argued for. It is the thesis of this study that in this, as in so many
other issues, Maimonides (1138–1204) went against the grain. Maimonides,
it will be shown here, affirmed, not the superiority of the moderns (the scholars of his and subsequent generations) over the ancients (the Tannaim and
Amoraim, the Rabbis of the Mishnah and Talmud) but the inherent *equality*
of the two. The equality spoken of here is not equality of halakhic authority,
but equality of ability, of essential human characteristics.

Throughout this work, I use the term "Rabbis" to refer to the Tannaim
and Amoraim, known in the Tradition as *Hazal* ("our Sages of blessed memory"). I transliterate Hebrew without diacritical marks. I have taken the liberty of occasionally emending the translations I cite here without, in every
instance, calling attention to that fact. Quotations from the Babylonian
Talmud are taken from the Soncino edition (London: 1935); those from the
Guide of the Perplexed are taken from the translation of Shlomo Pines
(Chicago: University of Chicago Press, 1963).

Some of the ideas discussed here were presented as a lecture during my
tenure as Visiting Professor of Religion at Northwestern University; I would
like to thank my colleagues there, especially Kenneth Seeskin, for their won-
derful hospitality and stimulating intellectual companionship. I worked
through many of the texts analyzed here with students in a seminar at the
University of Haifa. I would like to thank Oded Aloni, Sarah Cohen, Zvi Zitron,

and Gedaliah Oren for their many helpful and searching comments. A number of colleagues have been extremely generous with their assistance, reading the entire manuscript and commenting helpfully upon it. I extend my sincerest thanks to Ya'akov Blidstein, Shmuel Morell, David Novak, and Marc Shapiro. They have enriched the book, saved me from errors, and shown the true meaning of collegiality.

Small parts of this study have appeared in the following: "On the Status of the Astronomy and Physics in Maimonides' *Mishneh Torah*: A Chapter in the History of Science," *British Journal for the History of Science* 24 (1991): 453–63, and "Maimonides on the Science of the *Mishneh Torah*—Provisional or Permanent," *AJS Review* 18 (1993): 169–94. To their editors, my thanks for permission to reprint.

Introduction

This study deals with one facet of a subject central to Jewish self-understanding, but one which has received surprisingly little self-conscious attention, both within the Tradition, and from a scholarly perspective. To what extent, and in what fashion are Jews bound to accept the opinions and pronouncements of religious authorities? There are those among today's traditionalist Jews who affirm that the decisions of earlier authorities are binding in every facet of life. In particular, it is claimed that the Tannaim and Amoraim, that is, the Rabbis of the Mishnah and Talmud, have the authority to make determinations (in matters of Halakhah and otherwise) which are binding upon all subsequent generations. This authority is connected to the special character of the Rabbis themselves. In effect, it is claimed that because of certain innate characteristics, characteristics which have since disappeared from the human race, the Rabbis were blessed with an insight into Torah and human nature which made their decisions about both errorless.

In its strongest sense, the claim is thus made that there is no area of human life or thought in which the Tannaim and Amoraim can be wrong. On the face of it, this claim is problematic, since the Tannaim and Amoraim were notoriously prone to disagreeing with each other on almost every possible subject. The issue I wish to analyze here, however, concerns the relationship of subsequent generations to the Rabbis, and not the relationship among the Tannaim and Amoraim themselves.

One can argue, on the other hand, that the authority of the Rabbis has nothing to do with their own inherent characteristics, but is rather a function of formal matters, involving, for example, historical or social factors.

Thus, we have two conceptions of the *nature* of rabbinic authority, the essentialist and formalist approaches. According to the first view, there is an essential characteristic (or set of characteristics) which sets the Rabbis apart from all other humans and in consequence of which they are given by God the authority to make determinations binding on subsequent generations. On the "formalist" view, one can agree that the Tannaim and Amoraim have the authority to make determinations binding on subsequent generations, but deny that this authority flows from any special characteristic essential to their nature; rather, their authority derives from the role they played in Jewish history.

Let me illustrate the distinction with an example. In the system of constitutional law binding in the United States, the framers of the U.S. Constitution have a kind of authority which, in normal circumstances, cannot be limited or overturned. Independence Day rhetoric aside, no one seriously thinks that the "Founding Fathers" enjoy this authority because of their inherent superiority over subsequent generations of Americans. Rather, this authority is a _formal_ consequence of the system of law accepted in the United States. Similarly, one could accept the authority of the Rabbis, and agree that it is much more binding than that of the framers of the U.S. Constitution, without also affirming that the Tannaim and Amoraim are essentially or inherently different from and superior to you and me.[1]

A further distinction must be drawn. Accepting the authority of the Rabbis, on either the essentialist or formalist account, does not by itself determine the extent of that authority: does it extend to all areas of life and thought, or is it limited in its application? These limits can be drawn narrowly or broadly. On the narrowest interpretation, the authority of the Rabbis could be limited to technical questions of Halakhah. To that could be added areas like general Jewish values or theology for a somewhat broader but still limited interpretation. According to many contemporary interpreters of Judaism, however, the authority of the Talmudic Rabbis to make binding determinations extends to every area of life, including the natural sciences.[2]

We have spoken so far of the nature and limits of rabbinic authority. There is a third question which must be raised. What does it mean to say that the Rabbis have the authority to make binding determinations? Does it mean that what they say is always true and one who rejects (or maybe even questions?) their determinations is not only a heretic, but a damned fool besides? Does it mean, on the other hand, that what they say must be taken with utmost seriousness, and that only a damned fool would refuse to examine their statements in order to understand them in the best possible light? On this second view, one is not committed to accepting everything the Rabbis say about every subject, but one certainly treats their pronouncements with great respect. It is obvious that one's position concerning this third issue will be greatly affected by one's position concerning the first two. If one adopts an essentialist view of the nature of the authority of the Tannaim and Amoraim, and also claims that that authority extends to all areas of life and thought, one is forced to adopt the first of the two options outlined here, that what the Rabbis say is always true and any deviation from that truth is both heresy and foolishness.

On the basis of what we have analyzed thus far, we may distinguish several different senses of rabbinic authority. The strongest claim would be that the Rabbis are essentially different from and superior to subsequent generations, that their authority extends to all areas of life and thought, and that refusal to accept that authority as absolutely binding constitutes heterodoxy (not to mention stupidity). The weakest claim would be that the Tannaim and Amoraim are essentially like all normal human beings, that their authority derives from some formal characteristic, that it is limited to the area of technical questions of Halakhah, and that in all other areas one ought to treat their pronouncements with all due respect, but not necessarily as infallible.[3]

It is the thesis of this study that Maimonides accepts the authority of the Rabbis in the weak sense outlined here. In order to substantiate that claim, much attention will have to be given to the related claim that Maimonides does not adopt the notion of "the decline of the generations" (variously called *yeridat ha-dorot, hitkatnut ha-dorot,* or *hitma'atut ha-dorot,* the "dimunition" or "decline of the generations"), according to which each succeeding generation, or each succeeding epoch, is in some significant and religiously relevant sense inferior to preceding generations or epochs. Maimonides' views on the subject of rabbinic authority cannot be addressed without first examining this idea, an idea as we shall see, often used to bolster the claim that Tannaim and Amoraim have authority in the strong sense. Much of this study will be given over to showing that Maimonides does not hold this notion.

Since Maimonides nowhere treats these issues explicitly, his views will have to be derived indirectly from his writings.[4] Included among the issues that need to be analyzed are Maimonides' periodization of halakhic history, his attitude towards the scientific pronouncements of the Rabbis (and of Aristotle), his understanding of the nature of science and of scientific truth, Maimonides' understanding of progress in the sciences, his attitude towards his contemporaries and predecessors, his approach to the issue of the settled order of nature, and many others.

It is important to stress that in claiming that Maimonides accepts the authority of the Tannaim and Amoraim in the weak sense only I am not claiming that he rebelled against an already well-entrenched view, according to which rabbinic authority should be understood in the strong sense. On the contrary, Maimonides' position on this issue (unlike his position on many others) is not at all revolutionary.[5] It is only in the context of contemporary understandings of the authority of the Rabbis that Maimonides' position seems unusual. Furthermore, in denying that Maimonides held one of the generally accepted versions of the theory of the decline of the generations, I am not claiming that he consciously or unconsciously thereby rejected an aspect of rabbinic teaching. Indeed, it is the point of my first chapter to show that one cannot fairly claim that the notion of the decline of the generations was an aspect of the rabbinic world view to which Maimonides could have been expected to have allegiance.

But, on the other hand, it is by no means absurd to attribute a notion of decline to Maimonides. Not only does he make statements which lend themselves to the interpretation that he upheld some idea of the decline of the generations, but the idea *is* expressed in the Talmud, is held by some of his most illustrious predecessors, and was clearly adopted by many of his most prominent successors. This situation is illustrated through the analysis of some key medieval texts, and it is to this project that I devote the second half of chapter 1.

Maimonides' views on the nature of the rabbinic authority, and his associated failure to adopt a theory of decline, are connected to his Aristotelian understanding of the nature of nature, so to speak, and it is to a consideration of that issue that I devote the second chapter in this study. In showing the interdependence of philosophical, halakhic, and theological issues in Maimonides, I will be continuing a project to which I have devoted explicit attention over the last several years.[6] I take issue with those who, like Shlomo Pines, want to divorce Maimonides' philosophical concerns from his halakhic ones, demoting the latter to the status of an "avocation."[7] Just as I reject Pines' demotion of halakhah in favor of philosophy, I reject the opposed view which demotes Maimonides' philosophy in favor of his halakhah. This view is not popular in academe today, but it is held in circles where Maimonides is very closely studied and both demands and deserves serious refutation. By showing the intimate connection between Maimonides' views on various philosophical and scientific issues on the one hand, and his views on the nature of the authority of the Rabbis, on the other hand, I undermine the case of those who want to read Maimonides as if he were a classic representative of insular parochialism, as well as the case of those who wish to read him as a philosopher essentially divorced from Judaism.

Maimonides, admittedly, makes many statements throughout his writings which give credence to the claim that he did accept some notion of unavoidable intellectual and spiritual decline. These statements are described, analyzed, and explained in chapter 3. I show there that every Maimonidean text, which might be thought to reflect a doctrine of decline, can be better understood as describing historical and social reality, and not as describing the outcome of an ineluctable process of degeneration.

The next chapter in this study analyzes Maimonides' attitude towards rabbinic pronouncements on non-Halakhic matters. Maimonides consistently feels free to accept, modify, or reject these pronouncements; his only criterion is the extent to which they accord with the truth as he understands it. The freedom which he betrays in these contexts is inconsistent with any strong notion of rabbinic authority, and inconsistent with any version of the notion of the decline of the generations which accords the Rabbis an innately higher level of insight and understanding.

In chapter 5, I continue my argument by showing that not only did Maimonides not assume the decline of the generations, but he also actually assumed quite the reverse, that humanity marched upward, not downward. This point is illustrated with reference to Maimonides' views on the coming of the Messiah, on the nature of what we would today call "progress" in the sciences, on the increasing spiritual sophistication of human beings, and on the authority of later courts vis-à-vis earlier courts.

If Maimonides did not accept a strong version of rabbinic authority, and did not agree that the generations are declining, why did he accept the authority of the Rabbis? This subject is taken up in chapter 6, in which Maimonides' introduction to the *Mishneh Torah* is analyzed, and his understanding of the formal, not innate, character of rabbinic authority is elucidated.

Finally, in chapter 7, I seek to recast the argument of the book in terms of the way in which I came to understand it myself as opposed to the way in which I present it here. In so doing I attempt to come to grips with some of the contemporary issues which both grow out of its study and which served as its impetus. Readers more interested in the way in which rabbinic authority is conceived today than in Maimonides himself may want to begin with this chapter.

It will be useful, I believe, briefly to anticipate here some of the points made in that discussion. Readers whose acquaintance with Maimonides is colored primarily by the *Guide of the Perplexed* and the vast philosophical and scientific literature on which it depends, and readers whose acquaintance with Maimonides is colored primarily by the *Mishneh Torah* and the vast Talmudic and Gaonic literature on which it depends, often end up with a monochromatic and, to my mind, distorted view of the "second Moses." But even students of Maimonides such as myself, who strive for an integrated, holisitic view of his thought, are in danger of being led astray by unexamined assumptions. As described in greater detail below in chapter 7, I began the research on which this book is based with the assumption that Maimonides held an "essentialist" understanding of the authority of the Tannaim and Amoraim, but that he limited the *scope* of that authority to strictly halakhic matters. In matters of halakhah, I saw no reason to question the view regnant in traditionalist circles to the effect that Maimonides subscribed to some variant of the notion of the dimunition of the generations. In effect, the point of this book is to show not only that my assumptions were wrong, but why they had to be wrong.

CHAPTER 1

Decline of the Generations

In traditionalist Jewish circles the idea that the "generations" are diminishing has become something of a dogma, assumed and only rarely examined. Byron Sherwin expressed the idea very well:

"If the earlier scholars were like angels, then we [later scholars] are like human beings. However, if the earlier scholars were like human beings, then we are like asses." This Talmudic adage articulates the notion of progressive decline, which is assumed as a dogma of faith by much of classical Jewish literature. From this perspective, the further we move away from the revelation at Mt. Sinai chronologically, the weaker our spiritual and intellectual abilities become.[1]

This view is so pervasive in the Jewish tradition that even a scholar as sophisticated as Michael S. Berger can be led to write that "while the basic equality of all intellects is a tenet of the Enlightenment, a theological assumption of continually declining generations is a tenet of Judaism."[2]

The most restrained version of the doctrine holds that those who live in each successive historical epoch (however these may be defined) are inferior in spiritual and/or intellectual terms to those who live in preceding epochs. Here and there exceptions to the rule may appear—individuals whose abilities are such that they "should have been born" in an earlier period (R. Elijah Kramer, the Gaon of Vilna [1720–1797], is often cited as an instance of this phenomenon)—but by and large the rule obtains. The most extreme version of the doctrine holds that the decline is a persistent fact of human (or at least Jewish) experience and that each and every generation is literally inferior to its predecessors. On some views, as we will see below, this decline is qualitative, not just quantitative: according to the Maharal, for example, the Rabbis *as individuals* were essentially different from and vastly superior to later generations.[3]

This notion of the decline, or dimunition, of the generations is often used to explain the fact of halakhic history that Amoraim do not dispute Tannaim, Gaonim do not dispute Amoraim, Rishonim do not dispute Gaonim, and Aharonim do not dispute Rishonim.[4] While the connection between the two issues is often assumed to be rabbinic doctrine, it turns out to have been formulated explicitly for the first time only in the tenth century. But even that formulation is not self-conscious, systematic, or even particularly clear. Indeed, one of the points I wish to illustrate in this chapter is that the notion of the decline of the generations is not a doctrine susceptible of clear and precise statement. Indeed, it is hard to call it a doctrine at all, in the sense of a self-consciously articulated, systematic set of ideas.

I. **Talmudic Statements which Appear to Affirm the Doctrine of the Decline of the Generations**

There are several passages in the Babylonian and Jerusalem Talmuds which give expression to variants of the idea that later scholars were inferior to earlier scholars. As we shall see, these texts are not clear and certainly not consistent on the *nature* of the inferiority posited. Thus, in BT Shabbat 112b we read:

> R. Zera said in Raba b. Zimuna's name: If the earlier scholars [*rishonim*] were sons of angels, we are sons of men; and if the earlier scholars were sons of men, we are like the asses, and not even like asses of R. Hanina b. Dosa and P. Phinehas b. Jair, but like ordinary asses.[5]

In this passage, the earlier scholars remain unnamed and we are not told how many generations separate the earlier and later scholars. We are also not told in what the superiority of the earlier generations consists.

Such is not the case with respect to other passages, which are clearer on both questions. Thus, we find the following in JT Gittin 6.7:

> When Rabbi [Judah the Prince] wanted to raise a question about an opinion of R. Yose, he said, "Should we inferior folk raise questions about the opinion of R. Yose? For just as is the difference between most holy things and unconsecrated food, so is the difference between our generation and the generation of R. Yose." Said R. Ishmael the son of R. Yose, "Just as is the difference between gold and dirt, so is the difference between our generation and father's."[6]

R. Yose ben Halafta flourished in the middle of the second century (CE) and was active two generations before R. Judah the Prince; in several passages the latter expresses great respect for the former.[7] A number of issues come up in this passage: R. Judah feels inferior to R. Yose, apparently with respect to matters of halakhah; R. Judah generalizes his sense of inferiority and claims that his entire generation is inferior to that of R. Yose; this decline took place in a matter of two generations (according to R. Judah) or in a matter of a single generation (according to R. Ishmael).

The sense that later generations are intellectually inferior to earlier generations comes out clearly in another passage in the Yerushalmi, this one from Shekalim 5.1:

> Rabbi Haggai said in the name of R. Samuel ben Nahman: "The earlier ones plowed, sowed, weeded, scythed, hoed, harvested, sheaved, threshed, squeezed, separated, ground, sifted, kneaded, smoothed and baked while we have nothing to eat." R. Abba bar Yonah Zemina in the name of R. Ze'eira: "If the early ones [rishonim] were like angels, we are like humans; if they were like humans, then we are like asses." R. Mana said: "At that time [i.e., in connection with this] they said, we are not even like the asses of R. Phineas ben Yair."

R. Haggai's statement apparently means that despite all the preparatory work done by earlier scholars, we are incapable of taking advantage of what they have done. Our understanding of Torah is essentially inferior to theirs.

BT Eruvin 53a records a whole series of statements echoing this idea of intellectual decline:

> R. Johanan further stated: "The hearts [i.e., intellectual powers] of the earlier scholars [rishonim] were like the [twenty cubit wide] door of the *Ulam*, that of recent scholars like the [ten cubit wide] door of the *Heikhal*, while ours is like that of the eye of a fine needle." [By] earlier scholars [is meant the like of] R. Akiva; [by] later scholars [is meant the like of R. Akiva's student] R. Eleazar b. Shammua. Others say, [By] earlier scholars [is meant the like of] R. Eleazar b. Shammua; [by] later scholars [is meant the like of] R. Oshaia Beribi.[8] "While ours is like that of the eye of a fine needle."[9] "And we," said Abbaye, "are like a peg in a wall in respect to Gemara."[10] "And we," said Rava, "are like a finger in wax as regards logical argument."[11] "We," said R. Ashi, "are like a finger in a pit as regards forgetfulness."[12]

The difference between the earlier and later scholars in the first half of this passage is a matter of one or two generations; the quality of the difference clearly relates to the ability to master Talmudic texts and arguments.

Other sorts of decline seem to figure in our next two texts. BT Yoma 9b compares the reasons why the first and second temple were destroyed. It then says,

R. Johanan and R. Eleazar both say: "The former ones [*rishonim*] whose iniquity was revealed [by the prophets], had their end revealed [by the prophets, that they would return after an exile of 70 years], the latter ones [i.e., those who live after the destruction of the second temple] whose iniquity was not revealed have their end still unrevealed." R. Johanan said: "The fingernail of the earlier generations [*rishonim*] is better than the belly of the later generations." Said Resh Lakish to him: "On the contrary, the later generations are better, although they are oppressed by the governments, they occupy themselves with Torah." He [R. Johanan] replied: "The sanctuary will prove [my point] for it came back to the former generations, but not to the latter ones." The question was put to R. Eleazar: "Were the earlier generations better, or the later ones?" He answered: "Look upon the sanctuary!" Some say he answered: "The sanctuary is your witness [in this matter]."[13]

In this passage, the time differential is great: the roughly six hundred years that passed between the destructions of the two temples. The quality of the decline seems to be with respect to devotion to Torah, not the ability to study and understand it.

We find an apparently similar understanding of the decline of the generations in BT Ta'anit 24a–b:

> Rabbah once decreed a fast. He prayed but no rain came. Thereupon the people remarked to him: "When R. Judah ordained a fast, rain *did* fall." He replied: "What can I do? Is it because of studies? We are superior to him, because in the time of R. Judah all studies were concentrated on Nezikin, whereas we study all the six sections."

The text continues, describing how R. Judah found certain topics difficult, topics which were better understood in Rabbah's day. But despite the superiority of Rabbah's generation in matters of study,

> when R. Judah removed one shoe [as a sign of humiliation, preparatory to praying for rain], rain [immediately] fell; but when we cry out, no one pays heed to us. Is it because of some failing? If so, let any one knows of it, declare it. What, however, can the great men of a generation do when their generation [does not appear good enough to find favor in the eyes of God]?[14]

Here, the decline is explicitly *not* intellectual: in terms of rabbinic studies, the generation of Rabbah was superior to that of R. Judah. The decline appears to have been moral or spiritual, and, it should be noted, this decline characterized the masses of the generation, not its leadership who, apparently, felt themselves to be in no way inferior to R. Judah. The period of transition is apparently short: Rabbah's interlocutors seem to have been personally familiar with R. Judah's exploits. Moreover, if the Rabbah in question is Rabbah bar

Huna, and if the R. Judah in question is R. Judah bar Yehezkel (as seems to be the case), then they were more or less contemporaries, both of them having studied under Rav and Samuel.

A parallel to this text appears in Berakhot (20a), and there the decline is connected explicitly to matters of spiritual or religious significance. The story there is told about Abbaye; he was asked by R. Pappa, "Why is it that miracles were performed for those of former generations [*rishonim*], but no miracles are performed for us?" R. Pappa continues his question, arguing that the difference could not be that the former generations were superior in scholarship, proving his point with the same discussion found in Ta'anit 24a–b. The passage concludes with Abbaye's answer: "The former generations stood ready to martyr themselves for the sanctification of the divine name, we are not ready to martyr ourselves for the sanctification of the divine name."

A further passage in BT Berakhot (35b) sheds more light on rabbinic ideas concerning the decline of the generations:

> Rabbah b. Bar Hanah said in the name of R. Johanan, reporting R. Judah b. Ila'i: See what a difference there is between the earlier and the later generations. The earlier generations made the study of the Torah their main concern and their ordinary work subsidiary to it, and both prospered in their hands. The later generations made their ordinary work their main concern and their study of the Torah subsidiary, and neither prospered in their hands. Rabbah b. Bar Hanah further said in the name of R. Johanan, reporting R. Judah b. Ila'i: See what a difference there is between the earlier and the later generations. The earlier generations used to bring in their produce . . . [in such a way as to make it] liable to tithe whereas the later generations bring in their produce . . . [in such a way as to make it] exempt from tithe.

Rabbi Judah seems to be emphasizing the spiritual, religious superiority of the earlier generations (and the rewards of such spirituality).

The last passage I have found relevant to the notion that earlier generations are superior to later generations is from BT Yevamot 39b:

> We learned elsewhere: At first, when the object was the fulfillment of the commandment, the precept of levirate marriage was preferable to that of *halizah*; now, however, when the object is not the fulfillment of the commandment, the precept of *halizah*, it was laid down, is preferable to that of levirate marriage.

According to Biblical law, when a married man dies without children, his brother is expected to marry the widow; issue of that union are considered as descendants of the deceased. This is the meaning of levirate marriage. If the widow refuses to marry her brother-in-law a ceremony called "halizah" is performed. In earlier times, our text teaches, men took their brother's widows as wives solely in order to fulfill the commandment; in such circumstances levirate marriage ought to be performed. In later times, when men took their brother's widows as wives out of less honorable motives, _halizah_ takes precedence over levirate marriage. Here again, the emphasis is on spiritual elevation: early generations fulfilled God's commandments disinterestly, later generations for their own satisfaction.

The point is made even clearer in the sequel. Against the background of the point made in the text, Rami b. Hama said in the name of R. Isaac: "It was re-enacted that the precept of the levirate marriage is preferable to that of _halizah_." R. Nahman b. Isaac replied to him, "Have the generations become more fit?" and goes on to explain the reenactment of the precept of levirate marriage in terms of a particular halakhic debate, and not in terms of an improvement of the moral character of later generations.[15] Important for our purposes is the unarticulated assumption behind R. Nahman's question, that it is absurd to suggest that the generations have become more fit.

We have before us nine passages (a few of which appear more than once in the Talmudic corpus), reflecting the views of roughly a dozen rabbis.[16] With one exception, all the passages reflect a view of decline from generation to generation, not from period to period. The decline itself is manifested in both intellectual and moral/spiritual terms. What we do _not_ have is a settled doctrine proclaiming that every generation is necessarily inferior to its predecessors, or even a settled doctrine proclaiming that the scholars of any given historical period are necessarily inferior to the scholars of an earlier historical period. Nor do we have proof that some notion of decline informed the historical sense of all or most of the Rabbis.

II. Talmudic Statements Which Appear to Oppose the Doctrine of the Decline of the Generations

Systematic thinking and formulation, of course, are foreign to rabbinic thinking, and it would be surprising were we to find "settled doctrines" about anything.[17] My point here is that later generations of Jews have looked back into the Talmudic texts and found there the idea of the decline of the generations, an idea which they thought was explicitly accepted by all or at least the vast majority of rabbinic sages. What actually appears to have happened, however, is that scattered and apparently unconnected passages were understood by later interpreters as expressing a widely accepted and normative Tannaitic and Amoraic teaching. That is not to say that later interpreters read this teaching _into_ the Talmud; that is clearly not the case, since the texts we have described here do in fact exist. What these later interpreters seem to have done was read a systematic and consistent doctrine *out of* the Talmudic texts. But, as we shall see, as easily as one could derive the doctrine of the decline of the generations out of Talmudic texts, one can also derive an opposed doctrine from other passages.

It is, of course, established rabbinic practice that by and large Amoraim do not contradict Tannaim.[18] There does not appear to be any textual connection, however, between that *practice* and the idea that generations must necessarily decline. Given that there are other ways of explaining the periodization of Halakhah and the accepted practice that authorities in later periods do not contradict the positions of authorities in earlier periods (as will be discussed below), there is no necessary connection between the *idea* of the decline of the generations and the *fact* that later authorities hold themselves to be formally incompetent to contradict earlier authorities.

It is, indeed, entirely possible that the texts I have adduced here reflect nothing other than expressions of modesty, a quality very highly prized by rabbinic Judaism. They do not necessarily support the claim that the "decline of the generations" is a notion accepted by all or even a large proportion of the Rabbis. On the contrary, as I have stated, one can adduce texts which indicate the very opposite.

Two of these texts have already been cited: Rabbah's claim that his generation was superior to that of R. Judah in the study of Torah (BT Ta'anit 24a–b; BT Berakhot 20a, there attributed to R. Pappah), and Resh Lakish's argument with R. Yohanan (BT Yoma 9b). Other texts which lead to the conclusion that later generations can be as good as or even greater than earlier ones include Mishnah Eduyot I:5, " . . . no court may set aside the decision of another court unless it is greater than [the first] in number and wisdom . . ."[19] This text would make no sense were it impossible for a later court to be greater than an earlier court in *wisdom* and not just in number.[20]

BT Sukkah 28b tells the following:

> Our rabbis taught: Hillel the Elder had eighty disciples. Thirty of them were worthy enough for the divine presence to have rested upon them as upon Moses; thirty of them were worthy enough for the sun to have stood still for them as it did for Joshua son of Nun; and twenty of them were intermediate. The greatest of them was Jonathan ben Uzziel, the least of them, Rabban Yohanan ben Zakkai. They said of Rabban Yohanan ben Zakkai that he did not leave [unstudied] Scripture and Mishnah, Talmud, halakhot and aggadot, details of the Torah, details of the Scribes, *a fortiori* [arguments] and analogies, calendrical calculations and *gematriot*, the speech of the ministering angels, the speech of demons, and the speech of palm trees, fuller's fables, fables of foxes, a great matter and a little matter. A great matter—the account of the chariot; a little matter—the discussions of Abbaye

and Rava. [All this,] in fulfillment of the verse, *that I may cause those that love me to inherit substance, and that I may fill their treasuries* (Prov. 8:21). If the least of them was like this, how much more so the greatest of them! They said of Jonathan ben Uzziel that when he sat and occupied himself with Torah, every bird flying above him burst into flame.

The point for our purposes here is that Hillel the Elder had thirty students as great as Moses and eighty students as great as Joshua. Clearly, the authors of this passage did not accept the idea of the decline of the generations!

Not surprisingly, if Hillel's students were compared to Moses, Hillel himself was also (BT Sanhedrin 11a):

> Once when the Rabbis were met in the upper chamber of Gurya's house in Jericho, a *bat-kol* was heard from heaven, saying: "There is one among you who is worthy that the Shekhinah should rest on him as it did on Moses, but his generation does not merit it." The Sages present set their eyes upon Hillel the Elder.

Hillel the Elder himself was as great as Moses; his generation was such, however, that his true greatness could not find full expression. From this text one can derive two contradictory claims: that the generations are in decline, since the generation of Hillel could not "support" his greatness; or, that the generations are not in decline, since Hillel the Elder had the same personal greatness as did Moses. Our next text, however, is much less ambivalent.
BT Sanhedrin 21b–22a compares Ezra to Moses:

> It has been taught: R. Jose said: Had Moses not preceded him, Ezra would have been worthy of receiving the Torah for Israel. Of Moses it is written, *And Moses went up unto God* (Exodus 19:3) and of Ezra it is written, *He, Ezra, went up from Babylon* (Ezra 7:6). As the going up of the former refers to the receiving of the Torah, so does the going up of the latter.[21]

Not only was Ezra as great as Moses (as indeed, was Hillel), but the fact that he did not bring the Torah was not "explained away" in terms of the inferiority of his generation. Since the Torah had already been brought, it could not be brought a second time. That is the entire reason that Ezra did not bring the Torah. There was no problem with this personal qualities and, apparently, no problem with those of his generation. The Talmud continues here, maintaining that Ezra prepared himself to bring the Torah as Moses had, and that even though he himself did not bring the Torah, he changed its script. There is certainly no notion of the decline of the generations here!

The same point can be inferred from another passage (BT Menahot 29b):

> Rav Judah said in the name of Rav, When Moses ascended on high he found
> the Holy One, blessed be He, engaged in affixing coronets to the letters [of
> the Torah]. Said Moses, "Lord of the Universe, who stays Thy hand [i.e.,
> who forces you to do this]?" He answered, "There will arise a man, at the
> end of many generations, Akiva b. Joseph by name, who will expound upon
> each tittle heaps and heaps of laws." "Lord of the Universe," said Moses,
> "permit me to see him." He replied, "Turn thee round." Moses went and sat
> down behind eight rows [of students and listened to R. Akiva teach]. Not
> being able to follow their discussion, he felt weakened, but when they came
> to a certain subject and the disciples said to the master, "Whence do you
> know it?" and the latter replied, "It is a law given to Moses at Sinai," he was
> comforted. Thereupon he returned to the Holy One, blessed be He, and
> said, "Lord of the Universe, Thou hast such a man and Thou hast given the
> Torah by me!" He replied, "Be silent, for such is my decree." Then said
> Moses, "Lord of the Universe, Thou has shown me his Torah, show me his
> reward." "Turn thee round," said He; and Moses turned round and saw
> them weighing out [R. Akiva's] flesh at the market-stalls. "Lord of the Uni-
> verse," cried Moses, "such Torah, and such a reward!" He replied, "Be
> silent, for such is My decree."

This dramatic passage, of course, teaches many things, and can be used to
derive insight into rabbinic attitudes towards diverse matters. One such issue stares us straight in the face: the passage has Moses saying that Akiva
was superior to him![22] On the face of it, then, Moses, at least, did not accept
the conception of the decline of the generations.

R. Akiva's greatness is also the subject of a passage in BT Sanhedrin 38b:

> ... What is the meaning of the verse, *This is the book of the generations of
> Adam* (Genesis 5:1)? It is to intimate that the Holy One, blessed be He,
> showed him [Adam] every generation and its expounders [of Torah], every
> generation and its Sages. When he came to the generation of R. Akiva, he
> [Adam] rejoiced at his learning, but was grieved at his death.[23]

Apparently, R. Akiva and his generation were in no way inferior to those who
had gone before them; on the contrary, they appear to have been superior!
The exact nature of R. Akiva's superiority is not made explicit in these
passages. In another passage (BT Gittin 5b) the superiority of later generations seems be a matter of technical halakhic abilities: "The earlier generations were not expert in [preparing a divorce] *lishmah*, but the later
generations are expert in *lishmah*." The term *lishmah* here means the

ability to prepare a divorce document (*get*) with the proper intention of executing it for this specific man and woman.

Our issue comes up indirectly in a passage in BT Sanhedrin 64a:

> Then they said, "Since the time is propitious, let us pray that the evil inclination [may likewise be delivered into our hands]." So they prayed, and it was delivered into their hands. They imprisoned it for three days; after that they sought a new laid egg for an invalid in the whole land of Palestine and could not find one. Then they said, "What shall we do? Shall we pray that his power be but partially destroyed? Heaven will not grant it." So they blinded it with rouge. This was so far effective that one does not lust for forbidden relations.

The Rabbis imprisoned the evil inclination; in consequence, the sexual urge was so diminished that even hens ceased laying eggs. The Rabbis had no choice but to release the evil inclination, but they first weakened it. "This was so far effective that one does not lust for forbidden relations." The point for our purposes is that later generations may be construed as morally superior to earlier generations in that they no longer lust for forbidden relations.

This text, of course, may be read in another way: despite the fact that earlier generations had strong sexual desires they still withstood temptation, thus proving their superiority. The reading of the passage offered here, however, is supported by another text from Sanhedrin (20a), another text written, it would seem, by individuals who did not accept the notion of the decline of the generations. The passage deals with individuals who had succeeded in withstanding female seductiveness:

> R. Samuel b. Nahmani said in R. Jonathan's name: What is meant by the verse, *Grace is deceitful, and beauty is vain, but a woman that feareth the Lord, she shall be praised* (Proverbs 31:30)? *grace is deceitful* refers to [the trial of Joseph];[24] *beauty is vain*, to Boaz;[25] while *a woman that feareth the Lord, she shall be praised* [refers] to the case of Palti, son of Layish.[26] Another interpretation is: *grace is deceitful*, refers to the generation of Moses;[27] *beauty is vain*, to that of Joshua; *a woman that feareth the Lord, she shall be praised*, to that of Hezekiah.[28] Others say: *grace is deceitful*, refers to the generation of Moses and Joshua; *beauty is vain*, to the generation of Hezekiah; *a woman that feareth the Lord, she shall be praised*, refers to the generation of R. Judah b. R. Ilai, of whose time it was said that [though the poverty was so great] that six of his disciples had to cover themselves with one garment between them, yet they studied the Torah.

The point of the first part of this passage is that sexual restraint *increased* through history from Joseph through Boaz to Palti. The point of the second is that devotion to Torah study *increased* through history from the generation of Moses through the generations of Joshua and Hezekiah, to that of R. Judah b. Ilai. The generation of Moses witnessed the miracles of the Exodus and theophany at Sinai; their devotion to Torah is not remarkable. Similarly with the generation of Joshua, which witnessed the conquest of the land. The generation of Hezekiah, on the other hand, despite suffering from foreign conquest, remained devoted to Torah study, but even they are inferior to the generation of R. Judah b. Ilai, who, during and after the Hadrianic persecutions, and in conditions of direst poverty, continued their devotion to Torah.

We have before us, then, ten passages from the Mishnah and Babylonian Talmud each of which can be reasonably interpreted as denying the claim that each generation or historical period is necessarily inferior to its predecessors.[29] Now I do not for a moment think that that was the explicit intent of those passages, but they would not have been written as they were had their authors accepted as settled doctrine the idea of the decline of the generations, or were the notion of decline a conception which underlay rabbinic approaches to the world.

I am fully aware of the fact that each of the passages here adduced as denying the notion of the decline of the generations could be interpreted so as to make it consistent with that idea. My point is that there is no reason to do that in the absence of evidence that the "doctrine" of the decline of the generations was widely accepted as settled rabbinic teaching. And that, as we have seen, is simply not the case.

There is a methodological issue which ought to be noted. I am not here interested in the question whether the authorities cited in the passages adduced above actually said the things attributed to them; nor am I interested in the question of whether the positions attributed to these authorities were actually held by them, or held by the later scholars who edited the texts of the Babylonian and Jerusalem Talmuds. The point that concerns us here is, what options were presented to a twelfth-century student of the Talmud like Maimonides? Did he have any reason to think that failure to adopt some variant of the doctrine of the decline of the generations would place him outside of the mainstream of rabbinic Judaism as it had developed to his day? My claim here is that Maimonides could (and, as shall be shown, did) accept the Talmud as authoritative without feeling constrained to accept as fact the decline of the generations. It is an issue on which the Talmud can be reasonably construed as presenting various options. To the extent that the Talmud has widely held doctrines, the idea of the decline of the generations need not be seen as one of them.

There is a second methodological issue which must be addressed as well, a propos of the notion of widely held rabbinic doctrines. As noted above, the Rabbis were not systematic thinkers. One could argue that the various texts which I have cited as showing that some of the Rabbis, at least, did not hold the doctrine of the decline of the generations, were actually each written for a specific purpose, and ought not to be used to derive any lessons concerning the position of the Rabbis as a whole or of individual rabbis on issues like the decline of the generations. Resh Lakish, for example, in the text from Yoma 9b analyzed above, could be interpreted as trying to encourage his listeners in hard times, praising them for their dedication to Torah. The story about Moses listening to the lectures of R. Akiva is clearly designed to teach a lesson concerning rewards in this world; to that end, R. Akiva's greatness must be emphasized.

This is, of course, true, but it cuts both ways: the texts cited above, which are used to prove that the Rabbis held the doctrine of the decline of the generations, are no more evidence that the Rabbis held that position systematically than are the other texts proof that they did not. That is precisely my point: it is only by reading the Talmud from the vantage point of medieval and contemporary perspectives that we are led to assume that the Rabbis held the doctrine of the decline of the generations, even if only inchoately and unsystematically. To rephrase my position: no serious student of rabbinic literature would "accuse" the Rabbis of being systematic thinkers. Were I here seeking to refute the claim that the Rabbis held a clearly formulated doctrine of decline and applied it systematically, I would be arguing against a straw man. My argument is aimed at a more sophisticated but equally incorrect position, that the notion of decline informed the Rabbis' conception of their world, a world distinguished by its inferiority from that of the *rishonim*, the "earlier ones," of every and all preceding generations. I have argued here that to the extent that there is evidence which supports this claim, there is evidence of equal weight supporting the opposite claim, that the Rabbis' conception of their own world was not informed by any overall sense of decline.

III. Rav Sherira Gaon

Indeed, the first text in which the doctrine of the decline of the generations is presented as a fleshed-out ideology is the *Iggeret* of Rav Sherira Gaon (c. 906–1006). It is also the first text in which the decline of the generations is used as an explanation for the fact that Amoraim did not dispute Tannaim and that Gaonim do not dispute Amoraim.[30]

Let us examine the passages in which Rav Sherira expressly cites the notion of the decline of the generations.[31] In the first of these, he writes: "Rabbi Akiva sacrificed his life after the death of Rabbi Yossi ben Kisma. Rabbi Hananiah ben Teradion was executed and wisdom decreased [*ve-nitma'atah hokhmah*]."[32] In the next passage, R. Sherira explicitly connects the decline of the generations to Rabbi Judah the Prince's decision to compile the Mishnah:

> When Rabbi [Judah the Prince] saw such diversity in the teachings of the Sages, even though they all shared the same underlying principles, he feared that the teachings would not endure and would be lost. He saw that understanding [*lev*] was diminishing, the well springs of wisdom were being blocked up, and the prince [or angel] or Torah was disappearing. It is as they say, "If the earlier scholars were sons of angels, we are sons of men; and if the earlier scholars were sons of men, we are like asses"; and, as R. Johanan said, "The hearts [i.e., intellectual powers] of the earlier scholars were like the [twenty cubit wide] door of the *Ulam*, that of recent scholars like the [ten cubit wide] door of the *Heikhal* . . . [By] earlier scholars [is meant the like of] R. Akiva; [by] later scholars [is meant the like of R. Akiva's student] R. Elazar b. Shammua.[33]

Here R. Sherira connects two of the Talmudic passages cited above to justify his claim that Rabbi Judah the Prince noted an intellectual decline in his generation that prompted him, in part, to compile the Mishnah.

The comparison between the Amoraim and the Tannaim is made explicitly in the following passage:

> The hearts [of the earlier scholars] were wide,[34] and they only needed [to write down for themselves] the essential matters. However, when the Mishnah was completed and Rabbi [Judah the Prince] died, the heart diminished . . . they [the later scholars] included in the Talmud things which had not been necessary for the earlier scholars.[35]

This same comparison is extended in the last place in the *Iggeret* where Rav Sherira explicitly mentions our subject:

> "Along came the next generation and the heart became diminished, and matters which had been simple to the earlier [Sages] and which had been explained to their students, without the need to recite them and establish their exact wording in the Gemara became subject to doubt and they had to establish them in the Gemara with an exact wording . . . In each succeeding generation the heart became diminished as R. Johanan said in [Tractate] Eruvin, "while ours is like that of the eye of a fine needle"; Abbaye said, "We are like a peg in a wall in respect to Gemara"; Rava said, "we are like a finger in wax as regards logical argument." R. Ashi said, "we are like a finger in a pit as regards forgetfulness." As the heart diminished and doubts arose the explanations of the earlier [sages] which had not been established in their days were established and were studied."[36]

The Gemara was written because what had been simple to grasp on the part of the Tannaim was difficult for the Amoraim; the former had been able to teach their students without a text, the latter could not study without such a text.

Rav Sherira takes it as a matter of fact that earlier generations of Talmudic scholars had deeper understanding and greater wisdom than later generations. This decline is used to explain R. Judah the Prince's decision to compile the Mishnah and, by implication, the greater authority of Tannaim over Amoraim. Note should be made of the fact that Rav Sherira wrote his essay at the height of the Rabbanite-Karaite debate and may very likely have been influenced by that debate.[37] The polemical aspect of his work, defending the truth and authority of the rabbinic tradition, is thus seen more clearly. If this is true, it is significant for two reasons: (a) it supports my claim that Rav Sherira was the first to present the decline of the generations as a systematic ideology (doing so in response to the Karaite threat, not because the doctrine was clearly and explicitly held by his predecessors); and (b) it throws Maimonides' failure to adopt the doctrine into sharper contrast. Maimonides was well aware of the Karaite challenge and responded to it in a variety of ways.[38] The notion of the decline of the generations is a useful weapon in the armory of anyone fighting Karaism. That Maimonides failed to use it (as will be seen below) is significant.

The focus of our study is, of course, Maimonides. It is my contention that he rejects, or, more accurately, ignores the doctrine of the decline of the generations. Indeed, I will argue below that he cannot possibly accept it. This claim might surprise individuals familiar with the centrality of the doctrine for much of the halakhic world since Maimonides' day. I am trying to show here that the doctrine was less well established than is usually thought. The Talmudic evidence is ambivalent. Rav Sherira's letter may or may not have been known to Maimonides, but even if it was, there is no reason for him to have felt that its ideology bound him.[39] In brief, Maimonides was at most presented with the *option* of adopting some variant of the doctrine of the decline of the generations; it was an option which he chose not to adopt.

IV.   Other Medieval Statements

We could end our survey of texts expressing the doctrine of the decline of the generations here, and turn to Maimonides. It will be useful, however, briefly to see how the idea developed in Jewish literature contemporary and subsequent to Maimonides before examining his treatment (or, actually, non-treatment) of the idea. Doing this will put Maimonides' ideas in greater relief. I cite the following texts as examples only; they could easily be multiplied, but to no great advantage for our purposes.[40]

Rashi (1040–1105) seems to accept the idea of the decline of the generations as standard Jewish teaching in a number of his commentaries on the Babylonian Talmud. This comes out in his commentary on a well-known text in Makkot (23b–24a) which reads (in part):

> R. Simlai expounded: "Six hundred and thirteen precepts were communicated to Moses, three hundred and sixty-five negative ones, corresponding to the days of the solar year, and two hundred forty-eight positive ones, corresponding to the number of members of a human's body."

R. Simlai here tells us that the Torah contains precisely 613 commandments. We can skip the discussion which ensues, in which he proves his point. R. Simlai then continues his exposition, saying, "David came and reduced them [the six hundred thirteen commandments] to eleven." Here R. Simlai cites Psalms 15, in which he finds eleven characteristics of the person who seeks "to sojourn in the Lord's tabernacle and dwell in the holy mountain." The exposition continues; Isaiah is cited as having reduced the 613 to six, Micah to three, and Isaiah, again, to two. The passage ends as follows:

> Amos came and reduced them to one, as it is said: "For thus saith the Lord unto the house of Israel, Seek ye Me and live." To this R. Nahman ben Isaac demurred, saying [Might it not be taken as meaning,] Seek Me by observing the whole Torah and live? But it is Habakkuk who came and based them all on one, as it is said, "But the righteous shall live by his faith."

Rashi writes, s.v., *ve-he'emidan al ahat-esreh* (i.e., [David came] and reduced them to eleven): "In the beginning they [i.e., the Jews] were righteous [*zaddikim*] and could accept the yoke of many commandments, but the later generations were not so righteous and if they had to observe them all, you would find no meritorious man among them, and thus 'David came and . . . ' so that they would be considered meritorious if they fulfilled these eleven commandments [only]; similarly, in every period [*zeman*] the generations proceed downward and reduce it [i.e., the yoke of the commandments]." Here the decline is clearly presented in religious or spiritual terms.

In Rosh ha-Shanah 25b, the text of the Talmud reads, comparing 1 Sam. 12:6–11 (verse 11: *and the Lord sent Jerubaal, and Bedan, and Jeftah, and Samuel, and delivered you out of the hand of your enemies on every side*) and Psalms 99:6 (*Moses and Aaron among his priests and Samuel among them that call on His name*):

[We see therefore that] Scripture places three of the most questionable characters [Gideon, Samson, and Jephtah] on the same level as three of the most estimable characters [Moses, Aaron, Samuel], to show that Jerubaal [Gideon] in his generation is like Moses in his generation . . . to teach you that the most worthless, once he has been appointed a leader of the community, is to be accounted like the mightiest of the mighty. Scripture says also: *And thou shalt come unto the priests and the Levites and to the judge that shalt be in those days* (Deut. 17:9). Can we then imagine that a man should go to a judge who is not in his days? This shows that you must be content to go the judge who is in your days. It also says, *Say not, How was it that the former days were better than these* [i.e., that the judges in former days were better than those today] (Eccles. 7:10).

On this passage Rashi, *s.v., al tomar* . . . , comments *"For it is not out of wisdom that thou inquirest this* (Eccles. 7:10, continuation) since the [earlier] generations were better and more righteous than the latter, therefore were the former days better than these, since it is impossible for the latter to be like [i.e., as good as] the former." Here, again, the decline is spiritual, not necessarily intellectual.[41]

But Rashi also accepts the idea of intellectual decline: in Bava Mezia 33a, *s.v., ve-einah middah*, Rashi explains that the later Amoraim began writing down the Gemara because "hearts were diminished."[42]

Zohar III, 2a assumes the truth of the doctrine, applying it to the decline of Kabbalistic teachers, generation after generation.

Rabbenu Nissim ben Reuben Gerondi, in his *Derashot*, affirms that both wisdom and prophecy are emanated from God through the separate intellects to the soul. In both cases if an inferior individual associates with a superior individual, the former will acquire a greater level of emanations than he could otherwise:

This I take as a strong reason for the dimunition of prophecy and wisdom generation after generation, as is well known. . . . I take the reason for this to be that from Moses, peace upon him, to our day, all the prophets and sages, one after the other, are like a chain of causes and effects, which, as they continue to distance themselves from the first cause diminish in their degree, so is the matter equally [exactly?] with sages and prophets. For Moses, peace upon him, was caused in his wisdom and prophecy from the First Cause . . . and for this reason received these two emanations perfectly. Joshua received these emanations through Moses. . . . And so the prophets who follow Joshua.[43]

R. Moses b. Isaac Alashkar (1466–1542), Responsum number 53, strongly affirms the doctrine of the "diminishment of hearts," as he puts it, maintaining that the relation of his contemporaries to earlier generations is like that of apes to human beings. Given the halakhic context of his discussion, and the discussion itself, the issue seems to be primarily intellectual: subsequent generations are inferior in their ability to understand the thinking of earlier generations.[44]

R. Joseph Karo, in the Introduction to *Bet Yosef,* his commentary on the *Arba'ah Turim,* complains that in the course of time "we have been poured from vessel to vessel, dispersed and we have been subjected to continual and repeated tribulations." This sense of being at the end of a chain of transmission in which something is clearly lost (as happens when things are "poured from vessel to vessel") is reflected, it would seem, in R. Karo's halakhic decision-making.[45] In the *Shulhan Arukh,* Karo writes ("Laws of the Recitation of the Sh'ma," LXX.3):

> he who marries a virgin is released of the obligation of reciting Sh'ma for three days if he has not consummated the marriage [lit. "performed an act"] since he is pre-occupied with the performance of a commandment. This applied during the time of the early ones but nowadays, when other people [i.e., not newly married men] do not concentrate their intention [on the performance of commandments as they ought to], even he who marries a virgin recites [the Sh'ma].

This should be compared with the view of Maimonides, "Laws of the Recitation of the Sh'ma," IV.2:

> . . . One whose mind is preoccupied and in an agitated state because of any religious duty which he has to perform is freed from the obligation of reciting the Sh'ma.[46] Hence a bridegroom who has married a virgin is exempted from reciting the Sh'ma till he has consummated the marriage since his mind is not at rest, lest he not find her to be a virgin. If, however, consummation has been deferred till the night after the Sabbath subsequent to the marriage, it is his obligation to recite from the night after the Sabbath onward, for his mind has calmed down [*nitkararah da'ato*], and he is familiar with her, even though he has not had intercourse with her.[47]

This law as presented by Maimonides derives from BT Berakhot 11a; he is followed in his decision by the *Sefer Mizvot Gadol,* positive commandment 18, and by the *Arba'ah Turim, Orah Hayyim,* LXX.3. Maimonides in this case is the one following the tradition; R. Karo is the one changing the law because of the decline of the generations.[48] It should be noted, by the way, that for R. Joseph Karo the decline of the generations seems to involve spiritual, not necessarily intellectual decline: we no longer observe the commandments with the same level of intention and concentration achieved by our predecessors.[49] It should be further noted that the question debated between

Maimonides and R. Karo is one of *kavanah*, intention. On this more general question, Maimonides, unlike "his predecessors and contemporaries, recognizes no difference in the halakhic reality (and perhaps also not in human-pyschological reality) between his period and that of the Talmud."[50]

The most extreme expression of the doctrine of the decline of the generations that I have found in a premodern text is in the Maharal of Prague's Introduction to his *Be'er ha-Golah*.[51] Maharal says that it is very difficult for individuals properly to assess their worth. Proof of this is the fact that some people compare themselves to earlier generations with respect to wisdom and understanding. They justify this comparison on the grounds that all human individuals belong to the same species. The Rabbis, however, knew their own worth; Maharal quotes the passage from Eruvin to prove his point. Later scholars understood that the earlier scholars were

> entirely intellect; inasmuch as man [is composed] of body and intellect, in the earlier generations the intellectual faculty overpowered that of the body and had the upper hand, so much so that they had a heart wide enough [after Prov. 21:4] to receive wisdom, and they had no impediment from the body . . . the degree of contemporary men, [however,] is that of body, for [today] the body overpowers the intellect and the measure of the intellect['s ability to] receive is the measure of the eye of a fine needle.

Human beings[52] today, the Maharal continues, have the minimum level of intellect necessary to distinguish them from animals, but no more. The Maharal explains that Abbaye's comment about himself and his contemporaries, that they "are like a peg in a wall in respect to Gemara," refers to the deep intelligibles and sciences which can only be understood when taught by a teacher. "We, he says, "can only understand a very small bit of them; these deep intelligibles enter our hearts only in the way in which a peg enters hard wood, namely, that it enters it only very little." Rava's comment, that "we are like a finger in wax as regards logical argument," is taken by the Maharal to mean that our ability to reason is fuzzy. What little we learn he continues, explaining R. Ashi's comment that we "are like a finger in a pit as regards forgetfulness," we quickly and easily forget. The words of the earlier scholars, Maharal affirms, are like a "sealed book" to us, we do not and cannot really understand what they teach. The most we can hope to apprehend is how little we truly understand. If we appreciate that, then "we approach the degree of intellect." In sum, our generation is lacking in wisdom and empty of intellect. Here the emphasis is clearly on intellectual decline.[53]

R. Moses Hayyim Luzzatto derives a moral lesson from the fact of the decline of the generations:

> We see then that a man should not take credit to himself for the good that he
> does, least of all display vanity or pride on account of it. All this applies to
> men of the type of Abraham, Moses, Aaron, or David, or the other saints of
> whom we have made mention. But it hardly applies to us who are totally des-
> titute of merit. Our faults are so numerous that we do not need much think-
> ing to become aware of how unworthy we are. All our learning counts for
> naught. The most learned among us is no greater than the most insignifi-
> cant disciple of former generations. We ought to realize this fully, so that we
> may not become unwarrantably proud. Let us recognize that our mind is un-
> stable, that our intellect is extremely weak, that our ignorance is great, that
> error is rife among us, and that what we know amounts to very little. Pride
> hardly becomes us. Rather should we feel abashed and humbled.[54]

We, who are so dramatically inferior to Abraham, Moses, Aaron, and David,
in both intellectual and moral terms, have no reason for pride; we ought to
comport ourselves with appropriate humility.

The last text I wish to cite here was written near the end of the Jewish
Middle Ages by Hakham David Nieto (1654–1728). In many ways, it is the
most interesting. On the one hand Nieto expressly (and, I will try to prove,
correctly) maintains that Maimonides does *not* accept the doctrine of the
decline of the generations. On the other hand, he accepts it himself. For Maimonides as presented by Nieto, the Amoraim did not dispute with Tannaim
only because the latter received uncontroverted traditions from their teachers. The failure of the Amoraim to dispute the Tannaim has nothing to do with
the claim that the former were greater in number and wisdom. Nieto's own
view is that

> it is more correct to say that the Amoraim did not dispute the Tannaim
> because they [the Amoraim] recognized that they [the Tannaim] were
> greater than they in all respects, and not [only] because they had accepted
> upon themselves not to dispute, as the *Kesef Mishnah* wrote [explaining
> Maimonides, not expressing his own view].[55]

Nieto goes on to compare Abbaye in Berakhot 20a with Abbaye in Eruvin
103. In the former place, Abbaye, a fifth generation Amora, expresses the
superiority of himself and his colleagues over R. Judah, a second generation
Amora. In the latter text, Abbaye clearly expresses the inferiority of his generation when compared with earlier generations. Nieto solves the problem by
positing that Abbaye's basic doctrine is the decline of the generations as expressed in Eruvin; the other passage is to be explained in terms of the fact that
a dwarf sitting on the shoulders of a giant can see further than the giant.[56]

Before continuing with my discussion of Hakham Nieto, I should like
to digress to say a few words about the notion of "dwarves sitting on the

shoulders of giants." An indication of the diffusion of the idea of the "decline of the generations" is the wide-spread use of the parable of "dwarves on the shoulders of giants." Variants[57] of this expression are often used by later authorities to justify their divergences from the views of earlier figures. The earlier figures may have been giants, but we, even though we are dwarves, can, if perched on the shoulders of the giants, see further than they.[58]

Returning to Nieto, we find that he not only posits the decline of the generations, he also essays an explanation of the phenomenon:

> The diminishment of the heart which later generations attributed to themselves is not a function of diminishing intellect, but because of the abundance of troubles, [evil] decrees, and tribulations. The Kabbalists explain this in the reverse, but I do not concern myself here with secret teachings.[59]

Here Nieto, as we shall see, allies himself with what we shall see to be Maimonides' position: intellectual decline is a consequence of historical tribulations; it is not an unavoidable facet of human existence.[60]

In the present chapter, we have seen that the Talmud both supports and opposes the idea of the decline of the generations, that Rav Sherira Gaon turned it into a systematic doctrine which explains both the promulgation of the Mishnah and the superior authority of Tannaim over Amoraim, and that the doctrine became after Rav Sherira a standard aspect of Jewish self-understanding. It should be further noted that Rav Sherira, the Maharal, and Hakham Nieto all appear to have posited their claims concerning the decline of the generations in an attempt to "protect" the authority of the rabbinic tradition against contemporary attacks.[61] It is noteworthy that Maimonides, who faced the same Karaite assault on the rabbinic tradition as did Rav Sherira, as we shall see, did not use that tactic.

Against this background we can begin to attempt to understand Maimonides' attitude towards the decline of the generations, and through it, his attitude towards the nature and authority of the Tannaim and Amoraim.

CHAPTER 2

Maimonides
on Nature and Miracles

It will be shown below that Maimonides *did not* accept the ideas that
the Tannaim and Amoraim were supernaturally endowed with special qualities of wisdom, insight, and knowledge, and that all subsequent history is
marked by a process of moral, spiritual, and intellectual decline and decay.
Maimonides' position on these matters, which may be considered narrowly
"religious" in scope, depends upon his acceptance of an antecedent philosophical position, concerning the stability of nature and the possibility of
miracles. We can show, in other words, that he *could not* have accepted any
of the various notions of decline ordinarily assumed as authoritative in the
historical Tradition of Judaism.

I. The Stability of Nature

It is one of Maimonides' settled doctrines that nature is stable. In *Guide
of the Perplexed* II.28 (p. 335), for example, in the context of a discussion of
the indestructibility of the universe, Maimonides attributes to King Solomon
the doctrine that "these works of the deity—I mean the world and what is in
it—even though they are made [i.e. were created by God], are permanently
established *according to their nature* forever."[1] Maimonides attributes this
doctrine to King Solomon on the basis of Eccles. 3:14, *That whatsoever God
doeth it shall be forever; nothing can be added to it, not any thing taken from
it*. Maimonides explains:

> Thus he imparts in this verse the information that the world is a work of the
> deity and that it is eternal a parte post. He also states the cause of its being
> eternal a parte post; namely, in his words, *nothing can be added to it, nor
> any thing taken from it*. For this is the cause of its *being forever*. It is as if

> he said that the thing that is changed, is changed because of a deficiency in
> it that should be made good or because of some excess that is not needed
> and should be got rid of.

Maimonides understands King Solomon to be arguing that whatever God cre-
ates exists forever on the grounds that it would change (and ceasing to exist
is certainly a change!) only were it necessary to change, that is, only if God
had created the cosmos with some excess or deficiency. God's creation, however, is perfect and will thus last forever. Maimonides makes this explicit in
the continuation of the passage:

> Now the works of the deity are most perfect, and with regard to them there
> is no possibility of an excess or a deficiency. Accordingly, they are of neces-
> sity permanently established *as they are*, for there is no possibility of some-
> thing calling for a change in them.[2]

In sum, the world is created but everlasting, and all the types of creatures
in it will exist forever in the state in which they were created. There is no
possibility that they might undergo a change of essential nature. Were this
to occur, it would be an indication that God's original creation was defective
and had to be repaired.

The issue comes up again in *Guide of the Perplexed* (II.29), in the context of a discussion of prophecy and miracles:

> The notion toward which we are driving has already been made clear;
> namely, that the passing away of this world, a change of the state in which
> it is, or a thing's changing its nature and with that the permanence of this
> change, are not affirmed in any prophetic text or in any statement of the
> *Sages* either (p. 344).

There are three things which will not happen: (a) the end of the Universe;
(b) a change in the state of the Universe; and (c) a permanent change in the
nature of any particular entity within the Universe.

After explaining away rabbinic statements which seem to contradict his
thesis concerning the settled order of nature, Maimonides, as we saw in the
previous chapter, cites Eccles. 1:9, *There is nothing new under the sun*, in
support of his position.

So sure is Maimonides of the stability of nature, that he refuses to allow
biblical miracles to be interpreted as an exception to his claim:

> I have said that a thing does not change its nature in such a way that the
> change is permanent merely in order to be cautious with regard to the mir-
> acles. For although the rod was turned into a serpent, the water into blood,

and the pure and noble hand became white without a natural cause that necessitated this, these and similar things were not permanent and did not become another nature. But as they, *may their memory be blessed,* say: *The world follows its natural course* (p. 345).

Miracles are not suspensions of the settled order of nature: the changes they involve are temporary, and do not involve the transformation of a thing's essential character. We shall return to the question of miracles below.

In the context of a discussion of the difference between the Torah and other, non-divine, *nomoi*[3] Maimonides applies this idea of nature as stable and settled to human beings as well (*Guide of the Perplexed* II.40):

> Now as the nature of the human species requires that there be those differences among the individuals belonging to it and as in addition society is a necessity for this nature, it is by no means possible that [t]his society should be perfected—and this is necessarily so—through a ruler who gauges the actions of the individuals, perfecting that which is deficient and reducing that which is excessive.... Therefore I saw that the Torah, although it is not natural, enters into what is natural. It is a part of the wisdom of the deity with regard to the permanence of this species of which He has willed the existence, that He put into its nature that individuals belonging to it should have the faculty of ruling (p. 382).

For our purposes, the important points in this passage come at the end: the human species is permanent, and has a settled nature, instilled in it by God.

The stability of nature as construed here may also be important for Maimonides because of its connection to proofs for God's existence, unity and incorporeality. In *Guide of the Perplexed* I. 71 (p. 183), Maimonides writes, "I have already let you know that there exists nothing except God, may He be exalted, and this existent world, and that there is no possible inference proving His existence, may He be exalted, except those deriving from this existent taken as a whole *and from its details*" (emphasis added). I would like to suggest that we use this passage to interpret one of the last sentences in the first part of the *Guide* (I. 76, p. 31): "For the demonstrations by means of which all this [God's existence, unity, and incorporeality] can be made clear, can only be taken from the permanent nature of what exists, a nature that can be seen and apprehended by the senses and the intellect." The "details" of the existent world are apprehended by the senses. The nature of these "details" must be permanent for us to be able to prove the existence, unity, and incorporeality of God. A doctrine which posits instability (constant or episodic decline) in the nature of the human race undermines those proofs.[4]

This emphasis on the stable character of nature may also account for Maimonides' rejection of the idea that the great life spans achieved by some of the antediluvians reflected a general characteristic of human life in that era:

> As for the precise statements made by the text of the Torah regarding the length of life of certain individuals, I say that only that individual who is mentioned lived so long a life, whereas the other men lived lives that had the natural and usual duration. The anomoly in the individual in question may be due either to numerous causes attaching to his nutrition and his regimen or is due to a miracle and follows the laws thereof. It is not possible to say of this anything else.[5]

The implications for our purposes should be clear: to the extent that the doctrine of the decline of the generations involves the claim that the nature of human nature, so to speak, has undergone or is undergoing a change, Maimonides cannot accept it.

II. Miracles

There are two obvious ways in which this argument could be controverted: one could argue that Jews stand outside the settled order of nature and their decline is thus no violation of that order,[6] or one could argue that in every other way the Jews are part of the settled order of nature, but that the decline of the generations is simply a miracle.[7] The first possibility may be rejected out of hand; it is a position which would be acceptable to many Kabbalists, but is supported by no Maimonidean text I have ever seen, and is, moreover, opposed to many positions adopted by Maimonides, both explicitly and implicitly.[8] But Maimonides does affirm the possibility of miracles. Perhaps the decline of the (Jewish) generations is a miracle, involving as it does changes in the nature of at least one class of human beings? In order to disallow this possibility, we must examine Maimonides' understanding of miracles.

Maimonides discusses the nature of miracles in a number of places in his writings, but his most systematic and concentrated discussions are in his commentary to Avot, in the *Guide of the Perplexed*, and in his Treatise on Resurrection.[9] In the eighth of the "Eight Chapters" with which he prefaces his commentary on Avot, Maimonides argues with the "dialectical theologians" (i.e., the *mutakallimun*) who reject the claim that nature operates according to set rules implanted in it by God. "I have heard them say," Maimonides avers,

> [that divine] volition with respect to each thing takes place one moment after another, continuously. We do not believe that; rather, volition occurred during the *six days of Creation*, and [since then] all things act con-

tinuously in accordance with their natures. As [Solomon] said: *What is what will be; what has been done is what will be done; there is nothing new under the sun* (Eccles. 1:9). Therefore the sages insisted that there was a prior volition, during the *six days of Creation*, for all the miracles which deviate from custom and which have come about or will come about as has been promised. At that time the natures of those things were determined in such a way that was taken place in them would take place. When it takes place at the time it is supposed to, something new is presumed to occur, but that is not so. They expounded at length upon this subject in *Midrash Qohelet* and in other places. One of their sayings concerning this subject is: *The world follows is natural course*. In all that they say, peace be upon them, you will always find they avoid positing volition in each particular thing at each particular moment.[10]

God created the world by an act of will. Since then, all things act according to their natures with no further specific intervention by God. How, then, do we explain miracles? Maimonides cites a statement from the Rabbis to the effect that all miracles were installed in nature, so to speak, at the moment of creation. Miracles thus occur, not by specific divine intervention at the time they occur, but by prior arrangement.

Maimonides expands on this idea in his commentary to Avot proper (V.6):

. . . In the eighth chapter we mentioned to you that they [i.e., the Rabbis] did not accept that the divine will changes from time to time. Rather [they believed] that at the beginning of the fashioning of the phenomena, He instituted into their natures that through them there would be fashioned all that would be fashioned, whether the phenomenon which would be fashioned would be frequent, namely a natural phenomenon, or it would be an infrequent change, namely, a miracle. Therefore, he said that [at twilight] on the sixth day God instituted into [the nature of] the earth that Korah and his company would sink [into it], and concerning the well, that it would bring forth the water, and concerning the donkey, that it would speak, and similarly for the rest. . . . [11] Perhaps you will say that since all the wonders were instituted into the nature of these phenomena from the six days of creation, why then did he single out these ten? Know that he did not single them out in order to say that there is no other miracle which was instituted into the nature of the phenomena during the six days of creation except these. . . . [Thus,] by way of illustration, when the waters were parted on the second day, it was instituted into their nature that the Red Sea would be parted for Moses. . . . When the sun was created on the fourth day, it was instituted into its nature that it would stand still at that certain time when Joshua would address it. Similarly for the rest of the wonders.[12]

Here Maimonides adumbrates the same theory, adding examples: the Red Sea split because it was created such that at one point in its history it would split for Moses. On this understanding, miracles are not unnatural, but part of nature.

Maimonides' discussion of miracles in the *Guide of the Perplexed* is concentrated in II.29, in a passage we have already commented upon. In the context of a discussion of the parabolic nature of prophetic speech, Maimonides writes:

> The notion toward which we are driving has already been made clear; namely that the passing away of this world, a change of the state in which it is, or a thing's changing its nature and with that the permanence of this change, are not affirmed in any prophetic text or in any statement of the Sages either . . . [they hold] the view that nothing new will be produced in any respect or from any cause whatever (p. 344).

But if this is the case, what of miracles? Maimonides is quick to answer, in the *Guide of the Perplexed*,

> I have said that a thing does not change its nature in such a way that the change is permanent merely in order to be cautious with regard to the miracles. For although the rod was turned into a serpent, the water into blood, and the pure and noble hand became white without a natural cause that necessitated this, these and similar things were not permanent and did not become another nature. But as they, *may their memory be blessed*, say: *The world goes its customary way*. This is my opinion and this is what ought to be believed (p. 345).

Citing examples of three miracles worked by Moses, the greatest of the prophets, Maimonides says that they were indeed miracles, but involved no permanent changes, and certainly no essential change in the nature of the objects upon which the miracles were worked. Miracles do not involve permanent change in the nature of anything.

At this point in his discussion, Maimonides cites the theory which he had put forward in his commentary on Avot, here introducing it as "a very strange[13] statement about miracles," made by the Sages (*Guide of the Perplexed*, p. 345):

> This notion consists in their holding the view that miracles too are something that is, in a certain respect, in nature. They say that when God created that which exists and stamped upon it the existing natures, He put it into these natures that all the miracles that occurred would be produced in them when they occurred.

Whether or not Maimonides at this point accepts this theory, he certainly approves of the motivation of those who promulgated it, since

> it indicates the superiority of the man who made it and the fact that he found it extremely difficult to admit that a nature may change after the *Work of the Beginning* [*ma'aseh bereshit*] or that another volition may supervene after that nature has been established in a definite way (p. 345).

The "rabbinic theory" gives evidence to the discomfort felt by some of the Rabbis with the idea that nature might change after creation, or that God would intervene in the regular functioning of nature because of a new act of volition.

Maimonides continues by stating, "I have drawn your attention to the spirit of that passage and to the fact that all this serves to avoid having to admit the coming into being of something new." God created the world in the best possible way; after that creation, no thing or process established by nature will be subjected to permanent change, such change implying a defect in the original creation.

The discussion of miracles in *Guide of Perplexed*, II.29 is part of Maimonides' examination of the issue of creation. It is in that context that he summarizes his comments on miracles:

> The matter has now become clear to you and the doctrine epitomized. Namely, we agree with Aristotle with regard to one half of his opinion and we believe that what exists is eternal a parte post and will last forever with that nature which He, may He be exalted, has willed; that nothing in it will be changed in any respect unless it be in some particular of it miraculously (p. 346).

Aristotle had posited the eternity of the world in two directions: past and future. Maimonides accepted future eternity (that the cosmos will never be destroyed) but affirmed the creation of the Universe. But once created, the world has an "Aristotelian" flavor, and it "goes its customary way." Exceptions occur; these are miracles. Miracles, however, are temporary, onetime affairs; they never involve permanent changes in the nature of created entities.

The third text in which Maimonides discusses miracles at some length is his Treatise on Resurrection. Explaining why he interprets many messianic promises parabolically, Maimonides distances himself from the approach of the "masses" whom, he says,

> like nothing better, and in their silliness, enjoy nothing more, than to set the Law and reason at opposite ends, and to move everything far from the

explicable. So they claim it to be a miracle, and they shrink from identifying it as a natural incident. . . . But I try to reconcile the Law and reason, and wherever possible consider all things as of the natural order. Only when something is explicitly identified as a miracle, and reinterpretation of it cannot be accommodated, only then I feel forced to grant that this is a miracle.[14]

Maimonides tells us here that if things can be explained naturalistically, they should be explained in that fashion. For an event to be considered a miracle, it must satisfy two criteria: it must be explicitly identified as such, and no naturalistic explanation for it is forthcoming. As he says on the following page, "I shun as best I can changes in the physical order." Maimonides once again justifies his position by appealing to the rabbinic dictum, "the world follows its natural course."

In the closing pages of the Treatise on Resurrection, Maimonides returns to the issue of miracles, clarifying that miracles can occur within "the realm of the naturally impossible," such as changing a rod into a serpent (something which never happens in nature) or within "the realm of the naturally possible," such as the plague of locusts in Egypt. These latter are events which occur in nature, but "become miracles by one of three conditions or by all of them: (1) that the possible incident comes when the prophet says it will . . . (2) that the possible happening is singular and exceptional beyond anything imaginable of its kind . . . , (3) the duration and persistence of that possible event . . . "[15] Maimonides explains the first condition as involving cases where prophets precisely predict the occurrence of natural events (such as rain, or the collapse of an altar), the second as involving an unusual characteristic of a natural event (the plague of locusts in Egypt was unlike any before or since in its intensity; the pestilence in Egypt did not afflict the livestock of the Jews), and the third as involving the duration of events which usually occur as isolated incidents (such as the blessings and curses in Lev. 26 and Deut. 28).

Having established these parameters, Maimonides goes on to explain "that miracles in the naturally impossible class will not last at all," for if they did, people would come to doubt their authenticity: it would be suspected of a rod which permanently became a snake that it had been a snake all along. "Because of this fact," Maimonides continues, "I refuse to accept the duration of an unnatural situation . . . " Miracles involving naturally impossible events, therefore, are always isolated, one-time events.

But precisely the opposite pertains to respect of "the miracle in the class of the possible [which] is more wondrous the longer it lasts and endures." Thus, Maimonides says, concluding his discussion of miracles, he has no trouble accepting "the blessings that come from obedience and the maledictions on the community from disobedience unto eternity. For they become a sign and a portent, as I have pointed out."[16]

Maimonides makes it very clear that all things act in accordance with their inherent natures and that these natures are themselves stable; he maintains a static view of the cosmos. Permanent change in the nature of created entities is explicitly ruled out. The idea that human beings undergo a continuing decline in their moral, spiritual, and intellectual abilities in a miraculous way violates this understanding of nature. It also violates Maimonides' description of miracles, which are events which are explicitly identified as such, and for which no naturalistic explanation is forthcoming. The decline of the generations is nowhere identified as a miracle (certainly in no Biblical text, and not even in any of the rabbinic texts we analyzed above in chapter 1) and, to the extent that it occurs (something we shall see that Maimonides does not appear to accept), there are surely good sociohistorical explanations which should be sought before emulating the silliness of the masses, who seek to oppose Torah to reason.[17]

There is, furthermore, a kind of "double-bind" into which those who would want to claim that Maimonides affirms the miraculous nature of the decline of the generations get themselves into. To the extent that the entire process is miraculous, it must fall either into the realm of the naturally possible or the naturally impossible. Given that human society as a whole gives no evidence of intellectual decline (the technological and scientific breakthroughs of the contemporary world, including the marvelous little computer on which I am writing this book, render the need to argue for this claim otiose),[18] the decline of the (Jewish) generations must fall into the realm of the naturally impossible. But miracles in that realm, Maimonides explicitly holds, "do not last at all"; they are all brief, one-time events, not processes which last for thousands of years.

At this juncture it is important to quote the following from the *Guide of the Perplexed* III.50 (p. 616): "It is well known that it is impossible and inconceivable that a miracle lasts permanently throughout the succession of generations so that all men can see it." Maimonides goes on to cite the manna in the Wilderness, which nourished the entire Jewish people for forty years, as one of the greatest of the miracles of the Torah. The manna was one of the greatest miracles because it lasted for forty years. If the decline of the generations is a miracle, it would be a miracle which has lasted quite a bit longer than the forty years in the Wilderness! That alone makes it wildly unlikely that Maimonides would count it as a miracle. But since "it is impossible and inconceivable" that any miracle persist permanently, it is entirely and incontrovertibly clear that Maimonides would not and could not count the decline of the generations as a miracle.

Maimonides' conception of the stability of nature, and of the unchanging character of all created entities, militate against ascribing any variant of the theory of the decline of the generations to him; there is simply no way he could explain, consistent with his philosophical understanding of nature, a process whereby Jews became progressively and essentially less wise, less intelligent, less moral, and less spiritually adept. His conception of miracles is such that one cannot affirm that he holds that the generations thus decline in a miraculous manner.

In the present chapter we have seen why Maimonides cannot accept the notion of the decline of the generations. In coming chapters I will show that, despite common assumptions to the contrary, Maimonides indeed does not affirm the doctrine of the decline of the generations and refuses to ascribe to the Rabbis the sort of authority which would be rightfully theirs did he accept the theory. But first, we must turn to those texts which might be thought to indicate that Maimonides accepts some notion of decline.

CHAPTER 3

Maimonides on Decline

In the present chapter, I shall examine those of Maimonides' statements which might be thought to indicate that he accepted some variant of the decline of the generations. I will show that while Maimonides had a very pessimistic view of the period in which he lived, this pessimism was not a reflection of his acceptance of the doctrine of the decline of the generations, but, rather, reflected his assessment of contingent historical reality.

I. Maimonides on the Degradation of His Times

Maimonides clearly felt that he lived in degraded times, and gave frequent expression to the feeling. In one of his earliest compositions, his commentary on the Mishnah, Maimonides quotes one of the rabbinic texts ordinarily associated with the idea of the decline of the generations. Concerning the difficulty of understanding and accepting rabbinic homilies, he says:

> Therefore, we should judge all such [superficially unintelligible] homiletical expositions with a favorable predisposition, and deliberate well therein. Let us not be hasty in rejecting any one of them; rather, if one of their sayings is far [from comprehension] in our eyes, let us become proficient in the sciences until we understand their intentions in that matter, if our intellects can comprehend it. For the Sages had great desire to learn, and applied much understanding and effort [in the study of Torah], and avoided worldly pleasures, yet they would attribute a lack [of comprehension] to themselves, when they compared themselves to those that preceded them. And this is what they [meant when they] stated "The hearts of the ancients are like the door of the *Ulam*, but those of the later generations are not even like the eye of a fine needle." How much more so [does this apply to] us, since, with the loss of knowledge and wisdom, as God foresaw—*Therefore, behold, I will again do a marvelous work among this people, even a marvelous work and*

> *a wonder; and the wisdom of their wise men shall perish, and the prudence of their prudent men shall be hidden* (Isa. 29:14)—we have each of us had united in us four things: weakness of intellect, strong lust [for worldly pleasures], laziness in the quest for wisdom, and diligence [in attaining] worldly matters, the *four sore judgments* (Ezek. 14:21). How can we not but attribute deficiency to ourselves, when we compare ourselves to them?[1]

If the Rabbis were modest about their attainments, asks Maimonides, how can we not be even more modest? But does that mean that we are and must be innately inferior to the Rabbis? A second passage in the commentary on the Mishnah helps us to begin to understand Maimonides' position:

> And if the great Sages of the Mishnah, of blessed memory, regarded them [i.e., the laws of ritual purity] as difficult, how much more so we!.... Today, for our many sins, if you were to make the rounds of the heads of Israel's academies, not to mention the synagogues, you would find that this subject is difficult for them, every *halakhah* concerned with purity and impurity . . . and their like are difficult even for the great rabbis, and even more so for the students.[2]

The expression, "for our many sins," is a rabbinic idiom, but that is no reason to ignore it. Taking Maimonides literally here, what we have is the claim that the Jewish world in Maimonides' day had inferior leadership, not because that was the unavoidable fate of all generations after the Talmud, but because his particular generation did not deserve more.

There is a third passage in the commentary on the Mishnah in which our issue comes up. In his Introduction to the tenth chapter of Mishnah Sanhedrin, *Perek Helek*, Maimonides discusses three ways of understanding the *aggadot*, stories, of the Rabbis:

> You must know that the words of the sages are differently interpreted by three groups of people. The first group is the largest one . . . they accept the teachings of the sages in their simple literal sense . . . the members of this group are poor in knowledge. One can only regret their folly. . . . The second group is also a numerous one . . . [they understand the words of the sages literally as well and] ultimately declare the sages to be fools . . . this is an accursed group. . . . There is a third group. Its members are so few in number that it is hardly appropriate to call them a group, except in the sense in which one speaks of the sun as a group (or species) of which it is the only member.[3]

Most contemporary interpreters of the Sages, Maimonides tells us, are either fools or villains. A vanishingly small number of people read the stories of the Sages as they were meant to be read.

The critical attitude towards contemporary rabbinic leadership seen above finds expression in the Introduction to Maimonides' next major work, his *Sefer ha-Mizvot*:

> Such (unfortunately) is the mentality of even the elect of our times, that they do not test the veracity of an opinion upon the merit of its own content but upon its agreement with the words of some preceding authority, without troubling to examine that preceding source itself. And if this is true of the elect, how much more so of the populace.[4]

At first reading, this text seems to strengthen the claim that Maimonides accepted the doctrine of the decline of the generations. But in actuality, it proves quite the reverse. The weakness of the elect of his times is reflected precisely in its slavish adherence to "preceding authority." The truly elect examine preceding sources; they do not accept them simply because they date from an earlier period. Maimonides gives expression to this critique of his contemporaries in a letter he wrote later in his life, and to which we shall have recourse again below: "The great sickness and the *grievous evil* (Eccles. 5:12) consists in this: that all the things that man finds written in books, he presumes to think of as true—and all the more so if the books are old."[5]

The theme of the degenerate nature of the times in which Maimonides lived finds expression in the Introduction to the *Mishneh Torah*:

> In our days, severe vicissitudes prevail, and all feel the pressure of hard times. The wisdom of our wise men has disappeared, the understanding of our prudent men is hidden. Hence the commentaries of the Geonim and their compilations of laws and responses, which they took care to make clear, have in our times become hard to understand so that only a few individuals properly comprehend them. Needless to add that such is the case in regard to the Talmud itself—the Babylonian as well as the Palestinian—the *Sifra*, the *Sifri*, and the *Tosefta*, all of which works require, for their comprehension, a broad mind, a wise soul and considerable study, and then one can learn from them the correct practice as to what is forbidden or permitted, and the other rules of the Torah.[6]

The argument of this passage, I think, is fairly clear. "The wisdom of our wise men has disappeared, the understanding of our prudent men is hidden," *because* "in our days, severe vicissitudes prevail and all feel the pressure of hard times." It is historical circumstances, not irreversible changes in human nature, which make the wise and prudent inferior in their understanding of halakhic texts.[7]

The issue comes up again towards the end of the *Mishneh Torah*, in "Laws of the Sanhedrin," XXIV.2:

What has been said before constitutes a (fundamental) of Jewish law. But with the increase of courts whose members are lacking the requisite moral qualifications, and when even those whose conduct entitles them to the office do not possess adequate knowledge and understanding, most courts have decided not to transfer an oath (from the defendant to the plaintiff). . . . So too with other legal matters, it was decided that the judge should not be guided by his own opinion or that of one in whom he reposes confidence, lest any mediocre judge will say, "I believe it is so"; or, "I put credence in this man."[8]

Here Maimonides complains that courts in the generations preceding him have more and more been composed of individuals "lacking the requisite moral qualifications"; even when judges have those moral qualifications, then they do not possess adequate knowledge and understanding. This scathing criticism is offered without comment or explanation. It is a characterization of the times in which he lived, not an expression of a theory concerning the necessary degeneration of scholarship, wisdom, and morality. Maimonides does not exclude himself from these generalizations:

I am one of the humblest scholars of Spain whose prestige is low in exile. I am always dedicated to my duties, but have not attained to the learning of my forebears, for evil days and hard times have overtaken us and we have not lived in tranquillity; we have labored without finding rest. How can the Law become lucid to a fugitive from city to city, from country to country?"[9]

Here again, as in the Introduction to the *Mishneh Torah,* historical circumstances explain the decline. Maimonides "has not attained to the learning of [his] forbears," not because that is impossible due to the decline of the generations, but because "evil days and hard times have overtaken us and we have not lived in tranquility."

The elegaic quality of Maimonides' sense of his own times is indicated in the Introduction to the *Guide of the Perplexed* (pp. 16–17):

God, may He be exalted, knows that I have never ceased to be exceedingly apprehensive about setting down those things that I wish to set down in this Treatise. For they are concealed things; none of them has been set down in any book—written in the religious community in these times of Exile—the books composed in these times being in our hands . . . To sum up: I am the man who when the concern pressed him and his way was straitened and he could find no other device by which to teach a demonstrated truth other than by giving satisfaction to a single virtuous man while displeasing ten thousand ignoramuses—I am he who prefers to address that single man by himself, and I do not heed the blame of those many creatures . . .

In "these times of Exile" ignoramuses outnumber the virtuous by a factor of ten thousand to one. The times are such that an author must be apprehensive about teaching the truth. Maimonides' sense of living in degenerate times also comes up occasionally in his correspondence. Here is a clear example:

> As for yourselves, my esteemed friends, be confident and strong of heart! For alas, I am constrained to inform you that in these difficult days the people of your community and only a few of the neighboring communities stand alone in raising the banner of Moses and engaging in the study of the Talmud. Your people are preeminent in cherishing knowledge and wisdom. But in other communities in the East, the study of the Torah has ceased and especially is this true in most of the larger cities where a process of spiritual decay has set in. In all of Palestine there are only three or four Jewish places that have survived, and even they are spiritually impoverished. In Syria, as well, there is only the community of Aleppo where some scholars are still engaged in the study of Torah, although they are not prepared to sacrifice themselves for it. In the Babylonian Diaspora there are only two or three grapes [men of learning]: in Yemen and the rest of Arabia they know little of the Talmud save for having some superficial acquaintance with Aggadic expositions.[10]

The sense of being part of a "dying breed" so to speak, those who raise up the banner of Moses by engaging both in the study of Talmud *and* the pursuit of wisdom,[11] is clear in this sad text. Maimonides was sure that he lived in "spiritually impoverished" times. Maimonides' criticism of the "spiritual decay" in the communities of the East may reflect his well-known criticism of the contemporary Gaonate,[12] but that in no way diminishes the sense of spiritual, cultural, and intellectual impoverishment which pervades this letter and the other texts cited here.

None of this, however, proves that Maimonides felt that this spiritual, cultural, and intellectual decay was the result of ineluctable processes of decline which made each generation inferior to its predecessor, or each historical period less rich than its predecessor.

II. The Jews' Lack of Philosophical Sophistication

In a number of passages in the *Guide of the Perplexed*, Maimonides seeks to solve what for him had to have been a major problem, namely, the lack of philosophical sophistication among the Jews. This was a serious issue for Maimonides since he claimed that the Torah taught philosophy (roughly what we would today call science).[13] If the Torah was originally understood in that fashion, why did Jews in Maimonides' time not so understand it? Before turning to the solutions which Maimonides proposes for this problem, it will be useful to examine the issue itself in greater detail.

The first section of Maimonides' magnificent code of Jewish law, the *Mishneh Torah*, is called "Laws of the Foundations of the Torah." He opens that text with the following bold pronouncement: "The foundation of all [religious] foundations and the pillar of all the sciences is to know that there is a first existent." The basic teaching of religious faith, belief in God's existence, is equivalent to the most fundamental axiom of all the (Aristotelian) sciences, that God exists. In effect, Maimonides devotes the first four chapters of "Laws of the Foundations of the Torah" to working out the implications of this first sentence.

The first chapter is devoted to explaining and proving that God exists, is One, and is incorporeal. The second chapter opens with the command to love and stand in awe before God. Love and awe are emotions. How can they be commanded? Maimonides tells us that examination of God's works will lead one to love and awe. The central focus of the second chapter of "Laws of the Foundations of the Torah" is the separate intellects. These two chapters, Maimonides tells us at the end of the second one, are devoted to *"ma'aseh merkavah."*

"Laws of the Foundations of the Torah" III and IV are devoted to an exposition of the physical structure of the super- and sublunary worlds; their subject matter, Maimonides tells us, is called *"ma'aseh bereshit."* These four chapters together, we learn, were called *"pardes"* by "the ancient scholars."

The background to these gnomic assertions is a passage in the Mishnah. Hagigah II.1 places restrictions on the number and kind of people to whom one may teach certain matters: "One is not to expound upon forbidden sexual relations in the presence of three,[14] upon *ma'aseh bereshit* in the presence of two, and on the *merkavah* in the presence of one, unless he is wise and understands by himself . . . " The term *ma'aseh bereshit* is usually taken to mean the true meaning of the biblical accounts of creation at the beginning of the book of Genesis, while *ma'aseh merkavah* is understood as referring to the true meaning of the account of the chariot in the first chapter of Ezekiel.

In his commentary to the Mishnah here Maimonides says that the Rabbis call *ma'aseh bereshit* "the natural sciences and research into the beginning of the creation." Their intention in using the term *ma'aseh merkavah*, he says, is "the divine science, it being speech on existence in general,[15] on the existence of the Creator, His knowledge and attributes, that existent beings necessarily derive their existence from Him, the angels, the soul, the intellect which cleaves to man, and what comes after death." Maimonides explains that these sciences have to be restricted because, as he says, echoing the first line of Aristotle's physics, "it is known that every man by his nature desires all the sciences, whether he be foolish or wise." In other words, even the foolish seek to study these sciences. It is Maimonides' unstated assumption that exposure to these matters can be harmful to the foolish.

In the *Guide of the Perplexed*[16] Maimonides tells us once again that *ma'aseh merkavah* is identical with divine science: "Thus we have mentioned there [in the *Mishneh Torah*] that *ma'aseh bereshit* is identical with natural science and *ma'aseh merkavah* with divine science."[17]

Maimonides' exposition of Jewish law in all its myriad details, then, opens with an account of (Aristotelian) metaphysics and physics. These subjects are equated with what the Tannaim had called "*ma'aseh merkavah*" and "*ma'aseh bereshit*," subjects which these very same Tannaim had said could be taught only to a closed and small circle of initiates. *ma'aseh merkavah* and *ma'aseh bereshit* are further identified with *pardes*, the esoteric teaching of the Torah, a teaching so fraught with danger and difficulty that, as we are taught, of four great scholars who engaged in it, only one emerged unscathed.[18]

If the Torah originally taught physics and metaphysics, why were those subjects so little known by Maimonides' contemporaries, and why was he forced to write esoterically in a book devoted, in part, to showing that these subjects were indeed to be identified with *ma'aseh bereshit* and *ma'aseh merkavah*? In answering this question, Maimonides appeals, it might seem, to a variant of the doctrine of the decline of the generations.

III.   On the "Lost" Philosophical Tradition of the Jews

Religious revolutionaries in the Western monotheist faiths rarely identify themselves in those terms. Rather, they claim to be purifying the faith of disfiguring execressences which had grown upon the pure body of the religion. Anan, the founder of ninth century Karaism, did not proclaim himself as such; rather, he claimed to be reviving true normative Judaism, cleansing it of the illegitimate additions of the Rabbis. Martin Luther did not set out to create a new religion; he sought only to purge Christianity of the unauthentic trappings added to it by depraved Roman pontiffs. Hasidim claim that the first Hasidic Zaddik was not Rabbi Yisrael Ba'al Shem Tov, but Moses.

Similarly, Maimonides did not present himself as a religious revolutionary, seeking to import Greek philosophical ideas into the heart of Hebraic faith.[19] He claimed, rather, that these ideas had always been part of normative, historical Judaism. His philosophical work, therefore, was not innovative, but restorative. In the words of Leo Strauss, "he was merely recovering Israel's own lost inheritance."[20] Maimonides did not follow Halevi in claiming that all science originated with the Jews; as Isadore Twersky has argued, he "only" sought to situate philosophy as part of the original Torah, without denying that the ancient Greeks had independently arrived at similar understandings.[21]

Shlomo Pines is the foremost exponent of a school of thought which sees this Maimonidean claim as merely a "convenient fiction."[22] Since the interpretations of Maimonides offered in this study stand or fall independently of Pines, there is no need to explain why I reject his approach. For whatever it is worth, my own understanding is that Maimonides was wrong—the Written and Oral Torahs do not actually teach philosophy in an Aristotelian mode of course—but that he was sincerely wrong.[23]

All this is relevant for our purposes since Maimonides held that the Jews had "once cultivated the science of physics and metaphysics which they later neglected."[24] Is this neglect a sign of the decline of the generations? If it is not, then we further strengthen our claim that Maimonides was well aware of the fact of intellectual, moral, and spiritual decline, but that he attributed this decline to contingent, historical factors, not to an immanent, irreversible, entropic degeneration of the human spirit. Let us see precisely what Maimonides says on the subject.

He first raises the issue in his Commentary to the Mishnah:

> This fourth object [of Rav Ashi in editing the Talmud], that is, homiletical exposition as found in the Talmud, should not be considered as being of small virtue and little value. Rather, there is great depth therein, because it comprises remarkable intricacies and wonderful treasures. If one would rationally scrutinize these homiletical expositions, one would appreciate their incomparable excellence. These [expositions] reveal divine matters, as well as fundamental verities that learned Sages concealed and did not wish to disclose, and which [secular] philosophers spent generations [trying to understand]. If you will look into this [matter of homiletics] according to its simple sense, you will observe therein things that are exceedingly difficult to apprehend. They [the Sages] intentionally made this matter subtle and abstruse. One reason is to sharpen the thinking of pupils and to strengthen their hearts. Another reason is to blind the eyes of the foolish, so that they will never be enlightened in this matter. Similarly, some of the Sages did not wish to reveal the mysteries of wisdom to each other. . . . And when the Holy One, blessed be He, shall open the eyes of a man and reveal to him [some of the secrets], then he should conceal that which was revealed to him. . . . And if he does make a slight allusion to those [revealed] things, then he should present this allusion piecemeal to one whose intellect is full. . . .

Therefore, it is not proper for a wise man to divulge what he knows of these mysteries, save to one who is greater or equal [in wisdom] to him. . . . Furthermore, one should teach the masses of the people by way of epigrams and parables, so that it may be acceptable to women, youth, and children who, when their intellect has fully matured, will understand and comprehend the meaning of those hints.[25]

On the face of it, *aggadah* seems to be "of small virtue and little value."[26] This, however, is a mistake. *Aggadot* actually hide behind their facade intricate matters which philosophers have spent generations seeking to unravel. These matters must be kept secret to keep the foolish or the insufficiently prepared from being exposed to them.

If *aggadah* teaches in succinct and parabolic form that which philosophers strained to understand, then clearly the creators of *aggadah*, the ancient Rabbis of the Mishnah and Talmud, knew the truths which philosophers investigated and sought to comprehend. Philosophical teachings, however, are not appropriate for everyone and must not, therefore, be divulged to the masses lest the latter be harmed by exposure to ideas which are more likely to confuse than instruct them. The Rabbis thus chose, indeed, were forced to present their philosophical teachings in the form of stories and parables, that is, *aggadot*.

Maimonides characterizes the philosophical content of rabbinic *aggadot* as "mysteries." In hiding their philosophical teachings in this manner, the Tannaim and Amoraim were not innovating; they followed in the footsteps of the prophets. One of the purposes of the *Guide of the Perplexed*, Maimonides informs his reader in the Introduction to that work (p. 6), is "the explanation of very obscure parables occurring in the books of the prophets, but not explicitly identified there as such." The Rabbis, Maimonides goes on to tell us (p. 7) "following the trail of these books, likewise have spoken of them [physics and metaphysics] in riddles and parables."

In the text cited just above from the Introduction to the Commentary on the Mishnah (and certainly in the passage from the Hagigah commentary, cited briefly above), Maimonides expresses the idea that the ancient Rabbis were familiar with physics and metaphysics (largely as taught, independently, in Aristotelian philosophy), identified these subjects with the secrets and mysteries of the Torah known collectively as *pardes* and severally as *ma'aseh bereshit* and *ma'aseh merkavah*, and sought to hint at them in their aggadot.

Knowledge of these matters was once more widespread among the Jews than it was in Maimonides' own day. At the end of a discussion of certain astronomical phenomena, and a discussion of the nature and activities of the separate intellects, Maimonides points out he had already explained that all these views do not contradict anything said by our prophets and the sustainers of our Law. For our community is a community that is full of knowledge and is perfect, as He, may He be exalted, has made clear through the intermediary of the Master who made us perfect, saying *Surely, this great nation is a wise and understanding people* (Deut. 4:6). However, when the wicked from among the ignorant nations ruined our good qualities, destroyed our words of wisdom and our compilations, and caused our men of knowledge to perish, so that we again became ignorant, as we had been threatened because of our sins—for it says: *And the wisdom of their wise men shall perish, and the understanding of their prudent men shall be hid* (Isa. 29: 14); when, furthermore, we mingled with these nations and their opinions were taken over by us, as were their morals and actions . . . when, in consequence of all this, we grew up accustomed to the opinions of the ignorant, these philosophic views appeared to be, as it were, foreign to our Law, just as they are foreign to the opinions of the ignorant. However, matters are not like this.[27]

The Jews are, in their best state, "a community that is full of knowledge and is [therefore] perfect." When in such a state, Jews know that matters of physics (here astronomy) and metaphysics (here concerning the separate intellects) do not contradict *anything* taught by the prophets and other expounders of Torah (presumably, the Rabbis). When, however, the Jews become corrupted by "the wicked from among the ignorant nations," and thus lose their good qualities and wisdom, these debased Jews, "growing up accustomed to the opinions of the ignorant," then mistakenly believe philosophy to be foreign to the Torah.

We are certainly faced here with a doctrine of intellectual decline, but this decline is presented as an outgrowth of nothing other than historical circumstances which bring it about that Jews grow up "accustomed to the opinions of the ignorant."

This notion of growing accustomed to wrong thinking is the focus of another relevant passage from the *Guide of the Perplexed* (I.31, pp. 66–67):

Alexander of Aphrodisias says that there are three causes of disagreement about things. One of them is love of domination and love of strife, both of which turn man aside from the apprehension of truth as it is. The second cause is the subtlety and obscurity of the object of apprehension in itself and the difficulty of apprehending it. And the third cause is the ignorance of him who apprehends and his inability to grasp things that it is possible to apprehend. That is what Alexander mentioned. However, in our times there is a fourth cause that he did not mention because it did not exist among them. It is habit and upbringing. For man has in his nature a love of, and an inclination for, that to which he is habituated. . . . In a similar way, man has love for, and the wish to defend, opinions to which he is habituated and in which he has been brought up and has a feeling of repulsion for opinions other than those. For this reason also man is blind to the apprehension of the true realities and inclines towards the things to which he is habituated. This happened to the multitude with regard to the belief in His corporeality and many other metaphysical subjects as we shall make clear. All this is due to people being habituated to, and brought up on, texts that it is an established usage to think highly of and to regard as true and whose external meaning is indicative of the corporeality of God and of other imaginings with no truth in them,[28] for these have been set forth as parables and riddles. This is so for reasons that I shall mention further on.[29]

Once corrupted by wrong thinking, it is extremely difficult for humans to shake free of this corruption. Not only does any individual have "love for, and the wish to defend, opinions to which he is habituated and in which he has been brought up," but also, beyond that, we have a "feeling of repulsion for opinions other than those." Maimonides must make an argument of this nature: without it, it is hard to explain why Jews originally attuned to philosophical thinking have such a hard time throwing off the yoke of incorrect doctrines. Here again, the intellectual corruption of the Jews, and the persistence of that corruption, are explained in a purely naturalistic fashion, as the consequence of contingent historical factors which need not have happened.

That physics and metaphysics were originally known by the Jews is the burden of *Guide of the Perplexed* I.71 (pp. 175–76):

> Know that the many sciences devoted to establishing the truth regarding these matters[30] that have existed in our religious community have perished because of the length of time that has passed, because of our being dominated by the pagan nations, and because, as we have made clear, it is not permitted to divulge these matters to all people. . . . This was the cause that necessitated the disappearance of these great roots of knowledge from the nation. For you will not find with regard to them anything except slight indications and pointers occurring in the *Talmud* and *Midrashim*. These are, as it were, a few grains belonging to the core, which are overlaid by many layers of rind, so that people were occupied with these layers of rind and thought that beneath them there was no core whatever.

The philosophical sciences originally "existed in our religious community," but have disappeared for three reasons: (a) "the length of time that has passed", (b) the domination of the Jews by pagan (and thus morally corrupt and philosophically ignorant) nations, and (c) the fact which Maimonides has repeated in all the texts we have cited, that it is forbidden to reveal these matters in an open and public fashion. Any esoteric doctrine ("a few grains . . . overlaid by many layers of rind") taught to a restricted coterie of initiates over a very long period is in danger of being corrupted and forgotten; add to that the dislocations of exile and subjugation to violent and ignorant peoples, and it is no surprise that the original teaching has been lost. Against this background, can it be surprising that "these great roots of knowledge" disappeared from the nation of Israel? It would have been surprising had the philosophical sciences been preserved in these circumstances; there is no need to posit the decline of the generations to account for their disappearance.

The esoteric character of the philosophical teachings of the Torah would have been enough to account for their disappearance, even without the ravages of destruction and exile. This, it appears, is the burden of a passage in Maimonides' Introduction to *Guide of the Perplexed* III (p. 415):

> ... They have already made it clear how secret the *Account of the Chariot* was and how foreign to the mind of the multitude. And it has been made clear that even that portion of it that becomes clear to him who has been given access to the understanding of it, is subject to a legal prohibition against its being taught and explained except orally to one man having certain stated qualities, and to that one only the *chapter headings* may be mentioned. This is the reason why the knowledge of this matter has ceased to exist in the entire religious community, so that nothing great or small remains of it. And it had to happen like this, for this knowledge was only transmitted from one chief to another and has never been set down in writing.

The "account of the chariot" (*ma'aseh merkavah*) was meant to be kept very secret, perhaps because it was so "foreign to the mind of the multitude." Teaching it in public was forbidden; teaching it in private (as the Mishnah in Hagigah states) was permitted only in person, to one select student at a time; even then, the doctrine could not be divulged completely and openly—only an outline of it could be taught. This knowledge was meant to be esoteric, passed "from one chief to another," and never ever set down in writing.

All this being the case, it was almost a forgone conclusion that philosophy would soon be perceived as foreign to the Torah, a different species of wisdom altogether, rather than being understood as part and parcel of the Torah (III.54, p. 633):

> But since the rational matter in the Law is received through tradition and is not demonstrated by the methods of speculation, the knowledge of the Law came to be set up in the books of the prophets and the sayings of the Sages as one separate species and wisdom, in an unrestricted sense, as another species. It is through this wisdom, in an unrestricted sense, that the rational matter that we receive from the Law through tradition, is demonstrated. .... [The Sages hold that] the science of the Torah is one species and wisdom is a different species, being the verification of the opinions of the Torah through correct speculation.

The Torah teaches true doctrines. These doctrines can be demonstrated rationally. The sciences through which the true doctrines of the Torah are rationally demonstrated are, in actual fact, contained in the Torah, part of its very warp and woof. But because of all we have described these sciences have been incorrectly perceived as being different in quality from the Torah. It is one of the major purposes of the *Guide of the Perplexed* to show that this is not so, and that the Torah contains not just the expression of true doctrines, but their rational demonstration as well. Embedded in this passage we find once again Maimonides' doctrine that the esoteric character of the philosophic Torah caused it to disappear from the nation of Israel.

Jews in Maimonides' day are indeed degenerate when compared with those of their forefathers who understood the philosophic character of the Torah. Is that degeneration a consequence of the decline of the generations? Clearly not. It is the consequence of contingent historical factors. Do we know and understand less than our forefathers? Yes. Are we by nature inferior to them? No. It is Maimonides' claim and hope that we can be taught to recover our ancient intellectual heritage. That is the purpose of the *Guide of the Perplexed*. As we shall see below, it is also the point and purpose of messianism.

IV. Other "Historical Explanations" for Examples of Degeneration

In the previous sections, we have seen how Maimonides gave historical, formalist explanations for the authority of the Talmud *vis-à-vis* later generations and for the loss of the original, philosophical understanding of Torah revealed to Moses at Sinai. Eschewing appeals to the decline of the generations altogether, Maimonides seeks to account for these alterations without having to appeal to changes in human nature.

Maimonides clearly has a penchant for preferring what may be called historical explanations over theological explanations. We have had occasion above to examine Maimonides' attitude towards miracles. To Maimonides' mind it is no compliment to attribute to God direct miraculous intervention into the workings of nature and history. A truly competent God can create a world which does not need direct, immediate supervision and constant alteration; as Yeshayahu Leibowiz liked to put it, an efficient God does not need to be constantly pulling strings and pushing buttons. For Maimonides, the fewer miracles, the better. This is not a denial of providence, but a particular theory of providence.[31]

A. Defeat and Exile

A particularly vivid example of this approach is found in a famous letter which Maimonides sent to a group of scholars in Montpellier in response to a series of questions about the validity of astrology. In the course of his reply, an attack on astrology,[32] Maimonides makes the following illuminating comment:

> This is what led to the loss of our kingdom, the destruction of our Sanctuary, and extended the duration [of our exile] to the present day: our forefathers sinned and are no longer, in that they found many books concerning these matters of those who gaze at the stars—these things being the essence of idolatry, as we explained in "Laws of Idolatry,"[33]—they erred and were attracted to them, thinking that they were splendid sciences, having great utility and thus neglected the study of war and conquest, thinking rather that those [sciences] would be of use to them; for this reason did the prophets call them ignoramuses and fools. They were surely ignoramuses, *going after vain things which cannot profit* (1 Sam. 12:21).[34]

This text is really quite remarkable when seen against the background of traditional Jewish thought. "Because of our sins were we exiled from our Land and ousted from our country," is the way in which the prayer book explains the destruction of the Temple and the exile of the Jews from the Land of Israel.[35] Maimonides, of course, agrees. But what was the sin? The Jews sinned in forgetting how to defend themselves. This, in turn, was caused by their foolishly wasting their time on the study of astrology. Or, the Jews sinned by wasting their time with astrology instead of learning the arts of war. Either way, the Jews lost their independence and were forced into exile for precisely the same sorts of reasons which would bring any nation to lose its independence and be forced out of its homeland.

An event which the prayer book sees in strictly theological terms (sin and punishment) Maimonides sees in objective historical terms. For Maimonides also, of course, there is sin and punishment. But here the punishment is a direct and natural *consequence* of the sin, not a *response* of God's.[36] The destruction of the Temple, and the length of the exile are neither causes nor consequences of the decline of the generations; rather, the Temple was destroyed, the Jews exiled, and the exile continues all because of contingent, naturally explicable historical factors. *Olam ke-minhago noheg*, Maimonides liked to say, "the world follows its natural course"[37]; it is always preferable to explain natural and historical phenomena in terms of laws and processes which obtain universally.

B. Idolatry

We find another expression of this objective, naturalist, historical approach in Maimonides' explanation of the rise of idolatry. Given the biblical account of human creation, how can one explain the phenomenon of idolatry? Antediluvian humans, one would imagine, would have learned of God's existence from their forbears, Adam and Eve. This is surely the case for the descendants of Noah, a small group of persons whose very survival was a direct consequence of the saving providence of the One God. Yet, in the ten generations from Noah to Abraham belief in one God had been so completely wiped out of human consciousness that Abraham's devotion to his God is described as a great discovery.

In "Laws of Idolatry," I.1–2 Maimonides tries to account for this situation:

> In the days of Enosh, the people fell into gross error, and the counsel of the wise men of the generation became foolish. Enosh himself was among those who erred. Their error was as follows: "Since God," they said, "created these stars and spheres to guide the world . . . they deserve to be praised glorified, and honor should be rendered to them . . . and it is the will of God, blessed be He, that men should aggrandize and honor those whom He aggrandized and honored—just as a king desires that respect should be shown to the officers who stand before him, and thus honor is shown to the king." When this idea arose in their minds, they began to erect temples to the stars . . . their purpose, according to their perverse notions, being to obtain the Creator's favor. This was the root of idolatry. . . .

Maimonides goes on to explain that on the basis of this mistake human beings slowly forgot that God existed behind or beyond the stars and planets and began to worship these entities as gods.

Here again we see Maimonides trying to explain a process of degeneration without appealing to any innate or inherent quality of human beings. God was seen as being so powerful that the agents through which God works were also seen as worthy of worship. Once worship of these agents (the stars and spheres) had become established, God's sublimity and utter transcendence were further emphasized and it was ultimately forgotten that God exists behind and beyond the agents of divine will. These agents were then taken as gods in their own right: monotheism disappeared, replaced by idolatry.

Human beings became idolaters, then, because of a *mistake*, a well-intentioned mistake at that. They should never have simple-mindedly compared God to kings of flesh and blood (a comparison, I might note irrelevantly, fostered by the Jewish liturgy). This is a tragic mistake, but it is just that, a mistake, not the result of some unavoidable process of decline.

C. *Prayer*

We have before us a number of instances in which Maimonides analyzes instances of degeneration without recourse to the doctrine of the decline of the generations. Had he indeed accepted the doctrine, these are cases in which we would expect him to appeal to it. Our next example is particularly clear in this regard. Maimonides opens "Laws of Prayer and of the Priestly Blessing" with the claim that " . . . The number of prayers is not prescribed in the Torah. Nor is any form of prayer prescribed in the Torah . . . " (I.1). In the beginning, individuals were not expected to offer set prayers: "The obligation in this precept is that every person should daily, according to this ability, offer up supplication and prayer . . . " (I.2) The original intent of prayer was that each person should pray to the best of his or her ability and in accordance with their personal needs: "One who was fluent, would offer up many prayers and supplications. If one was slow of speech, he would pray as he could and whenever he pleased. Thus, also, the number of separate services depended upon an individual's ability . . . " (I.3).

By the time of the Mishnah, of course, set prayers were the norm. Had Maimonides accepted the notion of the decline of the generations he should have appealed to it here to explain the fact that Jews were no longer able to pray as originally intended. But here is his explanation:

> When the people of Israel went into exile in the days of the wicked Neb-uchadnezzar, they mingled with the Persians, Greeks, and other nations. In these foreign countries, children were born to them, whose language was confused. Everyone's speech was a mixture of many tongues. No one was able, when he spoke, to express his thoughts adequately in any one language, otherwise than incoherently . . . (I.4).

Jews can no longer pray eloquently; not because they are degenerate, but because of objective historical circumstances.

> Consequently, when anyone of them prayed in Hebrew, he was not able adequately to express his needs or recount the praises of God, without mixing Hebrew with other languages. When Ezra and his court realized this condition, they ordained the Eighteen Benedictions in their present order. (I.5)[38]

The inability of the Jews to express themselves in pure and elegant Hebrew, a prerequisite for proper prayer, made it necessary to establish set forms of prayer, notably the Amidah prayer. None of this has anything to do with the decline of the generations.[39]

D.   *"Small Matters"*

Isadore Twersky has drawn attention to a passage in the *Mishneh Torah* which raised the hackles of many readers of the work and sparked considerable debate. Twersky uses the passage in order to derive important lessons concerning Maimonides' attitude concerning the "nobility and superiority of metaphysics" relative to standard Talmudic studies.[40] Twersky is surely correct in his analysis; the passage is also important, however, as a further illustration of Maimonides' failure to adopt the doctrine of the decline of the generations.[41]

In chapter 1, I cited the following text from BT Sukkah 28b in order to show that the Talmud (in that passage at least) entertained the possibility that some of the Tannaim were of the same level as Moses and Joshua:

> They said of Rabban Yohanan ben Zakkai that he did not leave [unstudied] Scripture and Mishnah, Talmud, halakhot and aggadot, details of the Torah, details of the Scribes, *a fortiori* [arguments] and analogies, calendrical calculations and *gematriot*, the speech of the ministering angels, the speech of demons, and the speech of palm trees, fuller's fables, fables of foxes, a great matter and a little matter. A great matter—the account of the chariot; a little matter—the discussions of Abbaye and Rava.

In the *Mishneh Torah*, Maimonides makes fascinating use of this passage. In "Laws of the Foundations of the Torah," IV.13 we read,

> The topics . . . treated in the above four chapters are what our wise men called *pardes* . . . it is not proper to dally in *pardes* till one has first filled oneself with bread and meat; by which I mean knowledge of what is permitted and what forbidden. . . . Although these last subjects were called by the Sages "a little matter," for the Sages said, "a great matter—the account of the chariot; a little matter—the discussions of Abbaye and Rava," still they should have precedence. For the knowledge of these things gives composure to the mind at the beginning.

Maimonides takes the passage from Sukkah with what Twersky accurately calls "crushing literalism": Talmudic discussions are "a little matter," physics and metaphysics (the subjects of the preceding four chapters) are "a great matter."

How did other Jewish thinkers understand the passage in Tractate Sukkot? "The consensual explanation of this concluding passage," Twersky notes,

> . . . is that all the future queries of the Amoraim were crystal clear to Rabbi Johanan ben Zakkai and his Tannaitic colleagues. . . . Later generations . . . were marked by a decline in knowledge and insight and therefore had many sharp questions.

Twersky cites half a dozen sources in which this explanation is found. Maimonides ignores it altogether, as if it never occurred to him. The "small matters" were small in the days of the Tannaim and they remain small in Maimonides' day. There is no need to posit some process of decay or decline in order to explain that Talmudic deliberations are called "small matters."

V. Summary

Maimonides was convinced that he lived in degenerate times and gave repeated expression to that conviction. This attitude, however, he explained in terms of contingent historical circumstances, not in terms of the doctrine of the decline of the generations. In other instances where he would have been likely to appeal to that doctrine had he held it—the Jews' lack of philosophical sophistication, the destruction of the Temple, the rise of idolatry, the need for set prayers, the explanation of Sukkot 28b—he also appeals explicitly to historical circumstances, not some immanent process of decline, be it moral, spiritual, or intellectual. In the coming chapters, we shall examine other ways in which Maimonides' failure to adopt the doctrine of the decline of the generations and the idea that the Rabbis were essentially different from and superior to subsequent generations finds expression in his writings. We shall also see indications that far from seeing history as entropic, moving down as it were towards disorder and dissolution, he actually saw it as moving upwards, towards order and perfection.

CHAPTER 4

Maimonides' Attitude
towards the Authority of the Rabbis
in non-Halakhic Matters

I. Science

Maimonides clearly distinguishes between the role and authority of the Rabbis as transmitters of the Sinaitic revelation, as creators of Halakhah, as interpreters of the Torah, and as reporters of the best science of their day. With respect to the latter, at least, he clearly holds that the Rabbis can make mistakes:

> One of the ancient opinions that are widespread among the philosophers and the general run of people consists in the belief that the motion of the spheres produces very fearful and mighty sounds. . . . This opinion also is generally known in our religious community. Do you not see that the *Sages* describe the might of the sound produced by the sun when it every day proceeds on its way in the sphere?[1] . . . Aristotle, however, does not accept this[2] and makes it clear that the heavenly bodies produce no sound. You should not find it blameworthy that the opinion of Aristotle disagrees with that of the Sages . . . [The Sages themselves] in these astronomical matters preferred the opinion of the sages of the nations of the world to their own. For they explicitly say, "The Sages of the world have vanquished."[3] And this is correct. For everyone who argues in speculative matters does this according to the conclusions to which he was led by his speculation. Hence the conclusion whose demonstration is correct is believed.[4]

Truth is truth;[5] what is proved, is proved. No matter who says the opposite, their view is not to be accepted. Maimonides often gives expression to this attitude:

It is my intention in this chapter to draw your attention to the ways of research and belief. If anybody tells you in order to support his opinion that he is in possession of proof and evidence and that he saw the thing with his own eyes, you have to doubt him, even if he is an authority accepted by great men, even if he is himself honest and virtuous. Inquire well into what he wants to prove to you. Do not allow your senses to be confused by his research and innovations. Think well, search, examine, and try to understand [the ways of nature] which he claims to know. Do not allow yourself to be influenced by the saying that something is obvious, whether a single man is saying so or whether it is a common opinion, for the desire of power leads men to shameful things, particularly in the case of divided opinions. . . . I advise you to examine critically the opinions even of such an authority and prominent sage as Galen.[6]

One of the reasons that people are led astray by arguments to authority is because of their excessive veneration of the written word, especially when found in ancient works as we saw above: "The great sickness and the *grievous evil* (Eccles. 5:12) consists in this: that all the things that man finds written in books, he presumes to think of as true—and all the more so if the books are old."[7]

Maimonides rejects the approach; one must follow the argument where it leads, even if that means that one imputes error to one of the Rabbis of the Talmud:

I know that you may search and find sayings of some individual sages in the Talmud and Midrashoth whose words appear to maintain that at the moment of a man's birth, the stars will cause such and such a thing to happen to him. Do not regard this as a difficulty, for it is not fitting for a man to abandon the prevailing law and raise once again the counter arguments and replies [that preceded its enactment].[8] Similarly, it is not proper to abandon matters of reason that have already been verified by proofs, shake loose of them, and depend on the words of a single one of the sages from whom possibly the matter was hidden. Or there may be an allusion in those words; or they may have been said with a view to the times and business before him. . . . A man should never cast his reason behind him, for the eyes are set in front, not in back.[9]

We shall have occasion to return to this forthright statement below.

There is a second passage from the *Guide of the Perplexed* in which Maimonides informs his readers that the Rabbis erred on what we today call "scientific matters"; he explicitly distinguishes there the authority of the Rabbis as transmitters of Torah from their authority as astronomers:

Do not ask me to show that everything they [the Sages] have said concerning astronomical matters conforms to the way things really are. For at that

time mathematics were imperfect. They did not speak about this as transmitters of the dicta of the prophets, but rather because in those times they
were men of knowledge in those fields or because they had heard these dicta
from the men of knowledge who lived in those times. (III.15, p. 459)

Maimonides' position here, it is interesting to note, is reflected in a statement
made by his son, Rabbi Abraham:

The superiority of the Talmudic sages and the completeness of their qualifications in the exposition of the Torah, its details and the integrity of its
statements, in general and in detail—all this does not imply that we defend
and uphold their statements in matters of medicine, natural science, and astronomy, and to believe them as we believe them concerning the exposition
of the Torah, where they have the ultimate wisdom.[10]

Rabbi Abraham clearly distinguishes the authority of the Rabbis in matters
of "medicine, natural science, and astronomy," from their authority in matters of Torah. In this Rabbi Abraham accurately reflects his father's views; we
shall see below that Maimonides was less sure than his son that the Rabbis
have "ultimate wisdom" in all matters of Torah.

This attitude of Maimonides' towards the authority of the Rabbis in
scientific matters finds indirect expression in another source. In *Guide of
the Perplexed* II.9 (p. 268) Maimonides records the claim that there are nine
spheres. But spheres can be counted in different ways (compare "Laws of
the Foundations of the Torah," III.2) and what one person counts as nine,
another could count differently. "For this reason," Maimonides says, "you
should not regard as blameworthy" a rabbinic dictum which seems to indicate that there are only two spheres. Relevant to our theme here is the unarticulated supposition that in astronomical matters rabbinic dicta must be
brought into line with those of the astronomers, not the other way around.
It was the rabbinic dictum which might be thought to be "blameworthy,"
not that of the astronomers.

Our theme is found as well in *Guide of the Perplexed* III.37 (p. 544)
where Maimonides rejects the use of magic in medicine as forbidden *Amor-
ite usages* and then says,

You must not consider as a difficulty certain things that they have permitted, for instance, *the nail of one who is crucified and a fox's tooth*
[Shabbat 67a]. For in those times these things were considered to derive
from experience and accordingly *pertained to medicine* and entered into
the same class as it. . . . For it is allowed to use all remedies similar to
these that experience has shown to be valid even if reasoning does not
require them.

The apparent meaning of this passage is that the Rabbis *mistakenly*[11] believed that the nail of a crucified convict or a fox's tooth had medicinal value.[12]

Another indirect expression of Maimonides' idea that the Rabbis could err on matters of physics and metaphysics may be found in his use of the expression, "Ben Zoma is still outside," in *Guide of the Perplexed* III.51 (p. 619). As Marc Saperstein has shown in a remarkably sensitive reading of this passage in the *Guide*,[13] Maimonides uses this text (from Hagigah 15a) to indicate that Ben Zoma, a Mishnaic Sage, failed to attain mastery over the physical sciences and thus failed to attain even a rudimentary knowledge of God. Maimonides clearly felt that he himself was, and his student to whom he addressed the *Guide* could be, superior in their scientific (and hence religious) attainments to Ben Zoma. Ben Zoma, it should be recalled, was one of the three companions who sought to enter *pardes* with R. Akiba (Hagigah 14b). Ben Zoma apparently lost his mind as a result of this experience, adding to the impression that he would not have been considered by Maimonides to be one of the leading Rabbis.[14] This Ben Zoma passage will be analyzed again below in a different context, and in greater detail.

That Maimonides felt that the Rabbis could err in scientific matters is actually not surprising, since he also attributed such error to individuals who had reached a low level of prophecy and, it appears, to the Prophet Ezekiel himself. With respect to the first matter, Exod. 24 begins as follows: "And unto Moses He said: 'Come up unto the Lord, thou, and Aaron, Nadab, Abihu, and seventy of the elders of Israel; and worship ye afar off.' " After sundry events, the passage continues (verses 9–11):

> Then went up Moses, and Aaron, Nadab, and Abihu, and seventy of the elders of Israel; and they saw the God of Israel; and there was under His feet the like of a paved work of sapphire stone, and the like of the very heaven for clearness. And upon the nobles of the children of Israel He laid not His hand; and they beheld God, and did eat and drink.

These verses obviously raise all sorts of questions.[15] Let us focus here on one that troubled Maimonides: what does the reference to God's "feet" mean in this context? Just "seeing" God can be understood in purely intellectual terms;[16] but what could the reference to that which was under God's "feet" mean? Maimonides explains (I.5, p. 30) that it was "the nobles of the children of Israel," not Moses, who saw this. Their apprehension of God was imperfect because they were "overhasty [and] strained their thoughts," and thus "corporeality entered into" their apprehension of God to some extent. Put simply, they made a mistake in their approach to the science of metaphysics.

Now, who were these "nobles of the children of Israel?" From the verses themselves it appears that they are the "elders of Israel" spoken of earlier in the passage. This is the interpretation of the standard Jewish commentators on the Bible and, more important, it is clearly the interpretation of Maimonides himself as his discussion in I.5 makes clear. Who, then, are the elders of Israel? These "elders," it turns out, are individuals who, at least from time to time, reach a low level of prophecy. In *Guide of the Perplexed* II.45 Maimonides distinguishes eleven degrees of prophecy. The second degree is composed of those "who speak through the Holy Spirit."[17] The authors of Psalms, Proverbs, Ecclesiastes, Song of Songs, Daniel, Job, in short, of all of the Hagiographa, wrote their works having achieved this degree of prophetic inspiration. "It was to this group," Maimonides, says, "that the 'seventy elders' belonged" (with reference to Num. 11:25), as did Eldad and Medad, and as did all the High Priests when they received oracular information through the Urim and Tummim.

Not only could prophets of the second degree make mistakes in scientific matters, so, apparently, could prophets who had attained to the fifth degree of prophecy, prophets the like of Ezekiel. In his discussion of Ezekiel's vision of the chariot (*ma'aseh merkavah*), in *Guide of the Perplexed* III. 1–7, Maimonides seems to attribute to the prophet two views concerning astronomy which were incorrect: that the motions of the spheres make noises, and that the planets "Kokhav" and "Nogah" were above the sun. Maimonides is understood in this fashion by some of his medieval commentators and many of his modern interpreters.[18]

If as we see here Maimonides holds that individuals who achieved low levels of prophecy could err, how much more so would he hold that the Rabbis could!

II.   The Rabbis as Exegetes

Maimonides is, of course, extremely respectful of the Rabbis and, as we have seen, certainly accords them (formal, if not inherent) authority to determine Halakhah. That does not mean that he accepted their authority in all areas as such. We have seen that he felt comfortable in rejecting their scientific pronouncements. There is also evidence that he felt no compunction about not accepting their exegesis of biblical texts.

In his account of the messianic advent in "Laws of Kings and their Wars," in the last two chapters of the *Mishneh Torah*, Maimonides takes up certain rabbinic pronouncements concerning the order of the messianic advent. He writes:

> Some of our Sages say that the coming of Elijah will precede the advent
> of the Messiah. But no one is in a position to know the details of this and

similar things until they have come to pass. They are not explicitly stated by the Prophets. Nor have the Rabbis any tradition with regard to these matters. They are guided solely by what the scriptural texts seem to imply. Hence there is a divergence of opinion upon the subject.[19]

Some of the Rabbis make the claim that Elijah will reappear on earth before the coming of the Messiah himself. These Rabbis may or may not be correct, Maimonides says, but they are surely not promulgating a normative, binding belief of Jewish orthodoxy since "no one [not even the Rabbis!] is in a position to know the details of this and similar things until they have come to pass." Why is this the case? Details concerning the messianic advent "are not explicitly stated by the Prophets. Nor have the Rabbis any tradition with regard to these matters." The Rabbis of the Mishnah and Talmud may authoritatively interpret the words of Scripture *only* if these words are explicitly clear or if the Rabbis have a tradition concerning their proper understanding. Otherwise, the Rabbis "are guided solely by what the scriptural texts seem to imply." The Talmudic Rabbis, when describing the messianic world, were thus not transmitting "Torah from Sinai." They were, rather, reporting on what today would be called "educated guesses."[20] "Hence, there is a divergence of opinion upon the subject." Maimonides goes ahead to present his own exegesis of the verses, one for which there is very little precedent (to put it mildly!) in the tradition.

In explaining the verses of the Torah, therefore, not in the context of a homily with a moral or spiritual lesson, but in order to *teach* how the Messiah will come, the Rabbis present their own, private interpretations of those verses, interpretations which Maimonides has no compunction about rejecting or modifying. It is hard to believe that he would allow himself such a liberty did he accept the doctrine of the decline of the generations or attribute to the Rabbis authority to make determinations in matters not strictly halakhic.

III.   Criticism of the Rabbis

There are a number of passages in the *Guide of the Perplexed* where Maimonides voices reservations concerning opinions held or teachings promulgated by the Rabbis. Let us look at them in the order in which they appear.

In introducing a quotation from BT Berakhot 33b concerning appropriate ways of praising God, Maimonides takes an apparently unnecessary "swipe" at some the sayings of the Rabbis: "You also know their famous dictum—would that all dicta were like it . . . "[21] There seems to be no way of interpreting this passage other than according to its plain sense: Maimonides approves of this dictum of the Rabbis, while hinting at reservations concerning others.

Shem Tov in his commentary to this passage explains that Maimonides approved this dictum because, unlike so many other rabbinic texts, it does not present God in corporeal terms. In effect, he says that Maimonides did not give this passage his "seal of approval" at the expense of other passages in rabbinic literature; rather, Maimonides related to the fact that this passage taught in clear language what other passages taught parabolically, namely, that God was incorporeal.

I am not convinced that Shem Tov succeeds in removing the "sting" from this comment of Maimonides. In no other place with which I am familiar does Maimonides bemoan the fact that the Rabbis saw fit to couch their philosophical perceptions in misleading, corporealist language. If Shem Tov reads Maimonides correctly, then why, according to his understanding of Maimonides, did the Rabbis not teach true doctrines concerning God clearly and in every place? Clearly, they hid these doctrines because the had to. But then why not here?

No, I think that the conclusion cannot be avoided that Maimonides here is expressing approval for one rabbinic dictum and implied disapproval for other dicta of the Rabbis.

There is one passage in the *Guide of the Perplexed*, supported by a statement in one of his letters, in which Maimonides allows himself to disagree with the statement of one of the Rabbis because it is exactly that, a statement of *one* of the Rabbis, not a doctrine accepted by them all. Maimonides apparently felt that if a rabbinic dictum which he found problematic could be shown to be the opinion of only one of the Rabbis (what the tradition calls a *da'at yahid*), then there was no reason in the world why he had to accept it.[22]

Having established the indestructibility of the universe,[23] Maimonides writes (*Guide of the Perplexed* II.29, p. 344):

> The notion toward which we are driving has already been made clear; namely, that the passing away of this world, a change of the state in which it is, or a thing's changing its nature and with that the permanence of this change, are not affirmed in any prophetic text or in any statement of the Sages either. For when the latter say, "The world lasts six thousand years, and one thousand years it is a waste,"[24] [implying the destruction of the cosmos] they do not have in mind total extinction of being. For his expression, "and one thousand years it is a waste," indicates that time remains. Besides, it is the saying of an individual that corresponds to a certain manner of thinking.

Maimonides affirms here that several things will not happen: the universe will not be destroyed, the state of the universe as a whole will not be changed, nor will any particular class of individual entities have its nature permanently changed. Maimonides then cites as a counterexample a passage from the Talmud which seems to oppose the first claim, concerning the indestructibility of the created universe. He responds in a twofold fashion: first, the passage does not actually say that the universe will be destroyed, for even if the physical world is reduced to nothing, time remains; second, even if the intent of the passage is to affirm the utter destruction of the universe, this opinion is held by only one of the Rabbis, who affirms a doctrine which "corresponds to a certain manner of [apparently incorrect] thinking."

Having made these points, Maimonides goes on to argue in the following surprising fashion:

> On the other hand, you constantly find as the opinion of all Sages and as a foundation on which every one among the Sages of the Mishnah and the Sages of the Talmud bases his proofs, his saying: *There is nothing new under the sun* (Eccles. 1:9) and the view that nothing new will be produced in any respect from any cause whatever.

Strictly speaking, this argument appears to be a non sequitur: the verse from Ecclesiastes refers to the second and third issues raised by Maimonides, permanent change in the universe or in one of its components, not to the first, destruction of the universe as a whole.

However Maimonides ought to be understood here, he does not appear to be deciding an issue in terms of majority (favoring the indestructibility of the universe) over the minority (which favors the possibility of the universe's destruction). As presented by Maimonides there is no controversy here between two different approaches to the *same* question. Rather, we have opinions about two different questions. The first of these relates to the destructibility/indestructibility of the universe; the second to the possibility of permanent change within the universe. I am not sure why Maimonides does this. Perhaps he sought to hide the fact that the dismissed out of hand an opinion expressed by one of the Rabbis. Be that as it may, Maimonides here indeed summarily rejects the opinion of one of the Rabbis of the Talmud.

Maimonides, we see, had no apparent reservations about opposing his own positions to those of individual Rabbis. The issue comes up again in Maimonides' letter concerning astrology. Maimonides subjects "judicial astrology" (the use of astrology to predict the fates of specific individuals) to scathing criticism, calling its assertions "far from being scientific; they are stupidity." He continues,

> There are lucid, faultless proofs refuting all the roots of those assertions. Never did one of the genuinely wise men of the nations busy himself with this matter or write on it. . . . [25]

On the contrary, Maimonides goes on, the truly wise men of science mocked, scorned, and ridiculed those who gave credence to judicial astrology. The dispute between philosophers and followers of the true religion is not over astrology—all agree it is nonsense. Rather, the Jews affirm two "roots of the religion of Moses our Master" (p. 233), the first of which is denied by the philosophers: that what happens to an individual "is not due to chance, but rather to judgment." The second root, accepted by both the followers of Moses and by the philosophers is that "every action of human beings is left to them and that there is nothing to constrain or draw them"; that is, human actions are not predetermined.

Judicial astrology denies both roots, holding that everything that happens to us is determined by the stars. Astrology thus denies both chance and judgment on the one hand, and human freedom on the other. Astrology is thus both folly and falsehood. But there is a problem. "I know that you may search," Maimonides admits,

> and find sayings of some individual sages in the Talmud and Midrashoth whose words appear to maintain that at the moment of a man's birth, the stars will cause such and such to happen to him. Do not regard this as a difficulty . . . it is not proper to abandon matters of reason that have already been verified by proofs, shake loose of them, and depend upon the words of a single one of the sages from whom possibly the matter was hidden. Or there may be an allusion in those words; or they may have been said with a view to the times and business before him. (You surely know how many of the verses of the holy Torah are not to be taken literally. Since it is known through proofs of reason that it is impossible for the thing to be literally so, the author of the Targum rendered it in a form that reason will abide.) A man should never cast his reason behind him, for the eyes are set in front, not in back. Now *I have told you all my heart* [after Judg. 16:18] on this subject.[26]

Maimonides cannot deny that some of the Rabbis appeared to affirm the truth of astrology.[27] He offers several solutions to the problem, but under no circumstances is he willing to allow that this view of "some individual" Rabbis might be correct. The first solution is that the matter may have been hidden from the Rabbi in question (*she-nit'alem mimenu davar*). By that Maimonides can only mean that the individual Rabbi in questions may not have understood that astrology is false. The second possibility is that we must interpret the words of the Rabbis allegorically. The third possibility is the Rabbis meant what they said, but that they were not promulgating doctrine; they were, rather, reacting to a specific need or situation in a specific, onetime manner. It is with apparent respect to the second solution that Maimonides adds his remark (treated by Lerner, correctly in my view, as a parenthetical aside) concerning the need to interpret verses in the Torah allegorically.[28]

Maimonides' point appears to be that if we can interpret the words of the Torah allegorically to make them accord with reason, we can certainly interpret the words of the Rabbis allegorically in order to make them accord with reason. Whatever approach we adopt, Maimonides concludes, we must never be led astray and adopt incorrect views simply because they were held by Tannaim and Amoraim: "A man should never cast his reason behind him, for the eyes are set in front, not in back."

Maimonides makes a claim here worthy of our special attention. It is that there might have been Rabbis who incorrectly accepted the teachings of astrology. Note well: Maimonides has told us over and over again that these teachings are falsehood and folly, and contradict two of the "roots" of the Torah of Moses.[29] To claim that there were individual Rabbis who erred on these matters (and remember that Maimonides does not even try to pretend that only one of the Rabbis held astrological views) is to express an attitude of intellectual independence (not to mention superiority!) towards the Rabbis as individuals wholly at variance with any version of the doctrine of the decline of the generations. This text also clearly supports my interpretation of Maimonides, according to which the Rabbis have decisive authority in halakhic matters on formal grounds alone; that authority (an authority, it must be reemphasized, which Maimonides nowhere challenges) says nothing about their personal scientific attainments, as individuals, or as a group.

Maimonides appeared to be aware that the freedom he allowed himself in controverting the interpretations of the Rabbis might be controversial. "You should not find it incongruous," he writes in *Guide of the Perplexed* III.4 (p. 424),

> that, having mentioned the interpretation of Jonathan ben Uzziel, peace upon him, I propounded a different interpretation. You will find that many among the Sages, and even among the commentators, differ from his interpretation with regard to certain words and many notions that are set forth by the prophets. How could this not be with regard to these obscure matters. Moreover, I do not oblige you to decide in favor of my interpretation. Understand the whole of his interpretation from that to which I have drawn your attention, and understand my interpretation. God knows in which of the two interpretations there is a correspondence to what has been intended.

R. Jonathan ben Uzziel, a Tanna, is traditionally taken as the author of one of the Aramaic Targums to Scripture. Maimonides differed with one of his interpretations. He did not justify that difference by appealing to another tannaitic interpretation, a perfectly common and acceptable approach in these matters. No, he said that other Tannaim (and, I assume Amoraim) had felt free to disagree with R. Jonathan, as had certain unnamed but presumably post-Talmudic commentators on the Bible.

Maimonides goes on to say that he does not insist that his interpretation be preferred to that of R. Jonathan, concluding, however, with the assertion that "God knows in which of the two interpretations there is a correspondence to what has been intended." I take this to mean that Maimonides was convinced that his interpretation came closer to the original intent of the verses under discussion than did that of R. Jonathan. These verses, by the way, are from Ezekiel's vision of the chariot, the *ma'aseh merkavah*.

Be that last as it may, according to the plain sense of this passage, Maimonides, aware of the fact that differing with Tannaim on Biblical exegesis might not go down well with his readers, justifies himself that such freedom of interpretation is a constant of Jewish approach to the tradition. If I understand him correctly, he also claims that his interpretation is more correct (in terms of being closer to Ezekiel's original intent) than that of R. Jonathan. In other words, Maimonides implies here that he understood *ma'aseh merkavah* better than did the Tanna, R. Jonathan ben Uzziel.[30]

Our issue comes up again towards the end of the *Guide of the Perplexed*, in the context of the "parable of the palace" (III.51, p. 618):

> The ruler is in his palace, and all his subjects are partly within the city and partly outside the city. Of those who are within the city, some have turned their backs upon the ruler's habitation, their faces being turned another way. Others seek to reach the ruler's habitation, turn toward it, and desire to enter it and stand before him, but up to now have not yet seen the wall of the habitation. Some of those who seek to reach it have come up to the habitation and walk around it searching for its gate. Some of them have entered the gate and walk around in the antechambers. Some of them have entered the inner court of the habitation and have come to be with the king, in one and the same place with him, namely in the ruler's habitation. But their having come into the inner part of the habitation does not mean that they see the ruler or speak to him. For after their coming into the inner part of the habitation, it is indispensable that they should make another effort; then they will be in the presence of the ruler, see him from afar or from nearby, or hear the ruler's speech or speak to him.

In this parable, as he himself explains, Maimonides divides humanity into several categories: (a) those outside the city: subhumans holding no doctrinal beliefs whatsoever; (b) inhabitants of the city facing away from the palace: individuals holding incorrect doctrines; (c) inhabitants of the city seeking to enter the palace without yet having seen it: the masses of the Jews, "ignoramuses who observe the commandments" (p. 619); (d) those circling the ruler's palace, seeking a way in: "jurists [i.e., Talmudists] who believe true opinions on the basis of traditional authority, and study the law concerning the practices of divine service, but do not engage in speculation concerning the fundamental principles of religion and make no inquiry whatever concerning the rectification of belief" (p. 619). Members of this class, Maimonides further tell us, engage themselves in "studying mathematical sciences and the art of logic" (p. 619); (e) those who have entered the palace and walk around the antechambers: individuals who, unlike the previous group, "have entered into speculation concerning the fundamental principles of religion" and "understood the natural sciences" (p. 619); (f) those who have entered the inner court of the palace: the "men of [metaphysical] science . . . of different grades of perfection"; on of which grades of perfection is prophecy.

Maimonides here divides the inhabitants of the *polis* into those who hold incorrect doctrines, Jews who obey the commandments of the Torah without understanding, halakhists who study logic and mathematics, students of the fundamental principles of religion who have mastered physics, and, finally, the most intellectually perfected, those who have mastered metaphysics to varying degrees.[31]

In explaining this parable, Maimonides addresses R. Joseph ben Judah, the addressee of the *Guide of the Perplexed*, as follows:

> Know, my son, that as long as you are engaged in studying the mathematical sciences and the art of logic, you are one of those who walk around the house searching for its gate, as [the Sages], may their memory be blessed, have said resorting to a parable: "Ben Zoma is still outside." If, however, you have achieved perfection in the natural things, you have entered the habitation and are walking in the antechambers (p. 619).

Students of mathematics and logic, who have not yet mastered physics, are, like Ben Zoma, "still outside" and have not entered the ruler's palace.

"Ben Zoma is still outside" is part of an aggadah found in BT Hagigah 15a. The apparent meaning of the passage is that the Tanna R. Joshua ben Hananiah criticized his colleague Ben Zoma for not understanding *ma'aseh bereshit*, the account of creation. We have seen that Maimonides understands *ma'aseh bereshit* to be the rabbinic name for the science of physics. Those who do not know physics are "outside" of the ruler's palace.

Maimonides clearly hoped that his student would learn physics (as is clear from the direct address to him cited just above) and, perhaps, metaphysics.[32] In other words, Maimonides thought that his student (and he himself) were superior in their scientific (and hence religious) attainments to the Tanna Ben Zoma. Maimonides could not possibly have held this view of Ben Zoma while at the same time subscribing to the doctrine of the decline of the generations in any of the traditionally accepted senses of the idea.[33]

IV. Summary

Maimonides implicitly distinguishes among different roles played by the Tannaim and Amoraim, according them different levels of authority in their different roles. As transmitters of the Sinaitic revelation (and as creators of "fences" around that revelation as will become clear below in chapter six), the Rabbis as a class are, in effect, "always right." As scientists, however, they simply report on the best science of their day; sometimes they are right, sometimes wrong. In explaining the intent of biblical verses (at least on matters of eschatology), the Rabbis have no special authority (although there is no reason to suppose that Maimonides would deny that they have, by and large, profound insight). Maimonides, moreover, was not shy about disagreeing with some of the Rabbis, rejecting some of their teachings, or implying that some of them had reached only relatively low levels of scientific sophistication. Maimonides could not at one and the same time hold these views about the authority of the Tannaim and Amoraim and also accept idea that the Rabbis were as a class *essentially* superior to subsequent generations of human beings. Nor could he accept the corollary notion of the decline of the generations in any of its accepted meanings. Maimonides' (philosophical) views on the stability of nature render these (religious) positions unavoidable.[34]

CHAPTER 5

Maimonides on the "Advance" of the Generations

I. Introduction

In my analysis of Maimonides' attitude towards the authority of the Rabbis I have been concerned to show that he did not and indeed could not have subscribed to the doctrine of the decline of the generations, a doctrine which often lies at the heart of claims concerning the innate, inherent authority of the Rabbis. In the present chapter, I will bolster my argument by showing that not only did Maimonides not accept the theory of the decline of the generations, but he actually held the opposed view, that human beings are "progressing," rather than regressing.[1]

This is actually not such a surprising position for a Jew. Judaism, it may be said, is a process running between two poles, Sinai at one end, messianic redemption at the other end. The doctrine of the decline of the generations is predicated upon the view that Jews achieved their highest level of spiritual attainment at Sinai. From the heights of Sinai, only one direction is possible, down. The further removed we are from Sinaitic truth, the more pitiful our attempts to understand it. Perhaps the classic expression of this view is the midrash, "that a maid servant saw at the [splitting of the Red] Sea what Isaiah and Ezekiel and all the prophets never saw."[2] Israel's greatest prophets failed to attain the level of inspiration vouchsafed to the lowliest maid servant at the crossing of the Red Sea.[3] It is hardly surprising that circles in the Jewish world which emphasize the decline of the generations adopt a view of messianism which minimizes the role played by human beings in the messianic advent. Reaching messianic heights is only possible with God's direct intervention. Human attempts to forge a messianic reality are at best pathetically amusing, at worst the grossest blasphemy.[4]

If one views the messianic advent, however, as the culmination of a process to which human beings, unaided by overt miracles, make a decisive contribution, then one cannot possibly see spiritual history as an endless slide down a slippery slope, interruptible only by God's gracious intervention. If the Messiah is to come thanks to the concrete, this-worldly activities of human beings, then these humans must be capable of progressing towards the messianic world on their own steam. Human spiritual history is a history of progress, not decline. That progress can, of course, be interrupted, and backsliding is a constant danger, but the overall direction is onward and upward, not backward and downward.

In this chapter, we will see clear expressions of this approach in the writings of Maimonides. Our first, and most important discussion will relate directly to messianism.

II.   Maimonides on Messianic Progress

The coming of the Messiah is an issue to which Maimonides relates in almost all of his works. This is hardly the place to present a full-fledged account of his messianic teachings.[5] We will focus only on those aspects of his thought which impinge directly upon our question. In particular, I will show that Maimonides rejects all aspects of miraculous supernaturalism in his account of the coming of the Messiah[6] (thus making human contributions to it possible), that he views the messianic advent as a process occurring within history, subject to normal historical laws and circumstances, and further anticipates that the Messiah will come when humans have *brought* him, not when God *sends* him.[7]

Maimonides' first extended discussion of the Messiah is in his commentary to the Mishnah, in his introduction to the tenth chapter of Mishnah Sanhedrin, *Perek Helek*:

> The "days of the Messiah" refers to a time in which sovereignty will revert to Israel and the Jewish people will return to the land of Israel. Their king will be a very great one . . . all nations will make peace with him . . . and all countries will serve him out of respect for his great righteousness and the wonders which occur through him . . .

Maimonides introduces the "days of the Messiah" in direct opposition to the "world to come," a mode of purely spiritual existence enjoyed by the deserving after their deaths. The messianic era is emphatically this-worldly, not next-worldly. It is presented in entirely naturalistic terms. Do not be misled by Maimonides' comment concerning "the wonders which occur through" the Messiah, since he immediately clarifies:

However, except for the fact that sovereignty will revert to Israel, nothing will be essentially different from what it is now. This is what the Rabbis taught: "The only difference between this world and the days of the Messiah is oppression of one kingdom by another." In the days of the Messiah there will be rich and poor, strong and weak. However, in those days it will be very easy for men to make a living. A minimum of labor will produce great benefits . . . there will be sowing and reaping even in the Messianic time.

As will be seen below, this emphasis on the naturalistic nature of the messianic world is a motif which runs like a constant thread through all of Maimonides' writings on the subject.

Maimonides continues:

The great benefits which will occur in those days include our release from oppression by other kingdoms which prevents us from fulfilling all the commandments, a widespread increase of wisdom . . . , and the end of wars.

Freedom, wisdom, and peace, are not miracles. Rather, freedom from oppression allows the fulfillment of the commandments, which in turn leads to wisdom;[8] a consequence of widespread wisdom, of course, is peace. Wise people do not fight wars.[9]

Maimonides' naturalism finds further expression in the sequel:

But the Messiah will die, and his son and grandson will reign in his stead. . . . However his reign will be a very long one. All human life will be longer, for when worries and troubles are removed, men live longer.

Maimonides goes on to explain the stability of the messianic rule in naturalist terms: "There is no reason for surprise that the Messiah's reign [i.e., his dynasty's reign] will extend for thousands of years. As our Rabbis have put it: 'When good is gathered together it cannot be speedily be dissipated'."[10]

At the end of his Introduction to *Perek Helek* Maimonides presents his so-called Thirteen Principles. The twelfth of these "refers to the Messianic era." I would like to draw attention to one aspect of Maimonides' formulation: "We are to believe as fact that the Messiah will come . . . "[11] The belief demanded is in the coming of the Messiah, not that God will send the Messiah. Maimonides' formulation allows for the possibility that the coming of the Messiah depends upon factors in addition to God's inscrutable will, such as whether or not humans have acted so as to *bring* the Messiah.

The issue of the Messiah comes up twice in the *Mishneh Torah*, towards the beginning in "Laws of Repentance," and at the very end, in the last two chapters of the work, "Laws of Kings and their Wars," XI and XII. In "Laws of Repentance" IX, Maimonides again brings up the subject of the Messiah as a counterpoint to the true and lasting reward, the world to come. He once again emphasizes the this-worldly aspects of the messianic era and again explains the bountiful character of those times in terms of the wisdom which will be widespread.

Maimonides' most systematic account of messianism is presented in the "Laws of Kings" at the very end of the *Mishneh Torah*. Maimonides' decision to discuss the Messiah in this context is significant. The Messiah is presented as one of the legitimate kings of Israel; he is discussed within what may be called a "political" as opposed to "theological context." There were legitimate kings before him, and there will be legitimate kings after him. It is against that background that Maimonides writes:

> King Messiah will arise and restore the kingdom of David to its former state and original sovereignty. He will rebuild the sanctuary and gather the dispersed of Israel. All the ancient laws will be reinstituted in his days.[12]

The emphasis here is on the restoration of what was, not the creation of something new. This is significant in the context of the following passage (XI.3):

> Do not think that King Messiah will have to perform signs and wonders, bring anything new into being, revive the dead, or do similar things.

Quite simply, being a miracle worker is not part of the job description of the Messiah. This being the case, the restorative emphasis of XI.1 is better understood: creating a new and unprecedented world, ushering in a new dispensation, is beyond the capability of human beings. Since the messianic advent is not miraculous, it must involve the restoration of what was, not the creation of what has never existed. The messianic advent is best understood as a process which take place in discrete steps. The last stage of the process might be dramatically unlike the first stage, but no single intervening step in between is miraculous, or involves changes in quality as opposed to quantity.

Furthermore, the proof of the messianic pudding is in the eating thereof. The Messiah must *earn* his messianic spurs:

> If there arise a king from the House of David who meditates on the Torah, occupies himself with the commandments, as did his ancestor David, observes the precepts prescribed in the Written and Oral Torah, prevails upon Israel to walk in the ways of the Torah and to repair its breaches, and fights the battles of the Lord.

Maimonides clearly envisages the return of sovereignty to Israel *before* the advent of the Messiah. First Israel must have a king who satisfies certain criteria, as laid out here. If he satisfies these criteria, Maimonides continues, "it may be *assumed* that he is the Messiah." After that,

> If he does these things *and succeeds*, rebuilds the sanctuary on its site, and gathers the dispersed of Israel, [then] he is beyond all doubt the Messiah.

Maimonides' naturalism commits him to this hesitant, probationary approach to the Messiah. If the Messiah is not to perform any miracles then indeed it is impossible to know in advance if a putative Messiah is indeed the longed-for Redeemer. Only if he does what he is supposed to do can we be sure that he is the Messiah, and not a false Messiah, or someone who sought to be the Messiah and failed.

This aspect of Maimonides' messianic doctrine becomes clear in the immediate sequel, a text censored from all premodern editions of the *Mishneh Torah*:

> But if he does not meet with full success, or is slain, it is obvious that he is not the Messiah promised in the Torah. He is to be regarded like all the other wholehearted and worthy kings of the House of David who died and whom the Holy One, blessed be He, raised up to test the multitude, as it is written *And some of them that are wise shall stumble, to refine among them, and to purify, and to make white, even to the time of the end; for it is yet for the time appointed* (Dan. 11:35).

Can anything be clearer than this? A legitimate descendent of King David, sitting upon his throne in Jerusalem, would surely seek to accomplish what the Messiah is supposed to accomplish. If he succeeds, all the better; if he fails, he is certainly not to be blamed for the attempt. This is messianic naturalism with a vengeance.

The censored text continues with a remarkable passage:

> Even of Jesus of Nazareth, who imagined that he was the Messiah, and was put to death by the court, Daniel had prophesied, as it is written *And the children of the violent among thy people shall lift themselves up to establish the vision; but they shall stumble* (Dan. 11:14). For has there ever been a greater stumbling than this? All the prophets affirmed that the Messiah would redeem Israel, save them, gather their dispersed, and confirm the commandments. But he [Jesus] caused Israel to be destroyed by the sword, their remnant to be dispersed and humiliated. He was instrumental in changing the Torah and causing the world to err and serve another beside God. But it is beyond the human mind to fathom the designs of the Creator; for our ways are not His ways, neither are our thoughts His thoughts. All these matters relating to Jesus of Nazareth and the Ishmaelite [Mohammed]

who came after him, only served to clear the way for King Messiah, *to pre-pare the whole world to worship God with one accord*, as it is written *For then will I turn to the peoples a pure language, that they all call upon the name of the Lord to serve Him with one consent* (Zeph. 3:9). Thus the messianic hope, the Torah, and the commandments have become familiar topics—topics of conversation (among the inhabitants) of the far isles and many people, uncircumcised of heart and flesh. They are discussing these matters and the commandments of the Torah. Some say, "Those commandments were true, but have lost their validity and are no longer binding"; others declare that they had an esoteric meaning and were not to be taken literally; that the Messiah has already come and revealed their occult significance. But when the true King Messiah will appear and succeed, be exalted and lifted up, they will forthwith recant and realize that they have inherited nothing but lies from their fathers, that their prophets and forbears led them astray.[13]

Glossing this text in detail would take us too far afield. I will focus on only one aspect of it. The whole point of messianism for Maimonides as we shall see is to bring all human beings to the point where they abandon idolatry and embrace Judaic monotheism: the Messiah "will prepare the whole world to serve the Lord with one accord, as it is written, *For then will I turn to the peoples a pure language, that they may all call upon the name of the Lord to serve Him with one consent* (Zeph. 3:9)."[14] We learn here that thanks to the intervention of Christianity and Islam the world is being slowly "monotheized," thus making possible the eventual advent of the Messiah.

Why is this necessary? The coming of the Messiah is an expressly non-miraculous process. If the Messiah is meant to "prepare the whole world to serve the Lord with one accord," then the world must be made ready to accept belief in one God prior to the Messiah's coming. Converting the masses of the world from paganism to monotheism overnight, as it were, would be a miracle of impressive proportions! It is of necessity a miracle for, as Maimonides states, in another context, "a sudden transition from one opposite to another is impossible. And therefore man, according to his nature, is not capable of abandoning suddenly all to which he was accustomed."[15]

For the Messiah's advent to be possible, then, the world has to undergo a process of abandoning paganism in favor of monotheism. The population of the "whole world" has to become used to ideas such as Torah and commandments, and messianic fulfillment. In short, the Messiah can only come if the gentile nations progress towards deeper, fuller, and truer understanding of God. Given this state of affairs, for Maimonides to adopt the theory of the decline of the generations he would have to hold that Jews were subject to a process of unending decline while gentiles were subject to a process of unending ascent. Not very likely!

Maimonides opens chapter XII by reiterating his messianic naturalism:

> Let no one think that in the days of the Messiah any of the laws of nature will be set aside, or any innovation introduced into creation. The world will follow its normal course.

He closes the chapter, and with it the *Mishneh Torah* as a whole with the following words:

> In that era there will be neither famine nor war, neither jealousy nor strife. Blessings will be abundant, comforts within the reach of all. The one preoccupation of the whole world will be to know the Lord. Hence Israelites will be very wise, they will know the things that are now concealed and will attain an understanding of their Creator to the utmost capacity of the human mind, as it is written, *For the earth shall be full of the knowledge of the Lord, as the waters cover the sea* (Isa. 11:9).[16]

The whole world will be preoccupied with knowing the Lord. In such a world, it is no surprise that Jews, with the advantage of always having had the Torah, will be very wise, will know things that are now concealed (it is a safe assumption that Maimonides means *ma'aseh bereshit* and *ma'aseh merkavah*), and will achieve an understanding of God (i.e., perfection in metaphysics) to the very greatest extent that humans can achieve. All this will have to come about, as the opening of the chapter reminds us, through natural means.

Quite simply, for the messianic fulfillment to come about, a process of universal education will have to reach fruition, a process that depends upon no interruptions in the laws of nature or innovations in the natural world. Bringing the whole world to being preoccupied with nothing but the knowledge of God, bringing Jews to a particularly high level of that knowledge, can only happen through wide cooperation, hard work, and devoted study, over decades, perhaps generations.

Since, in the days of the Messiah, no "law of nature will be set aside" and no "innovation [will] be introduced into creation," this "monotheization" of the world must mark the culmination of a process which began before the Messiah's advent. The coming of the Messiah must mark the high point of human progress and ascent, not divine intervention to stave off ultimate degradation. As described in "Laws of Kings," Maimonides' doctrine of messianism makes it absolutely impossible that he could have accepted the theory of the decline of the generations.

III. Scientific Progress

Maimonides was no pollyanna, but we have just seen that he believed that human beings could and would make progress towards the messianic fulfillment.[17] He furthermore saw Christianity and Islam contributing towards that progress. Thus, Maimonides held that human history was largely marked by a development away from falsehood and towards truth, in matters both philosophical and religious.[18]

With respect to philosophical matters, let us look at Maimonides' understanding of the development of science since Aristotle. In a well-known letter to Samuel ibn Tibbon, Maimonides observes that there is no need for Samuel to study the writings of philosophers who preceded Aristotle because the works of the latter

> are sufficient by themselves and [superior] to all that were written before them. His intellect,[19] Aristotle's, is the extreme limit of human intellect, apart from him upon whom the divine emanation has flowed forth to such an extent that they reach the level of prophecy, there being no level higher.[20]

Aristotle, then, reached the pinnacle of non-prophetic human perfection. When we realize that Maimonides nowhere intimates that the Tannaim and Amoraim achieved prophecy, this becomes high praise indeed.[21] Aristotle achieved a level of human perfection as high as that achieved by the greatest of the Rabbis, assuming that any of them achieved it!

We must further note that in *Guide of the Perplexed* I.5 (p. 28), Maimonides calls Aristotle, "the chief of the philosophers."[22] Who were these philosophers of whom Aristotle is the chief? In his "Letter on Astrology" to the Rabbis of Montpellier, Maimonides writes that the *hakhamim*, wise men, of Greece, who were philosophers and "who are genuinely wise,"[23] never dealt with astrology. In his commentary to Mishnah Avodah Zarah IV.7, Maimonides explains at length that the philosophers never dealt with astrology which, as he explains both there and in "Laws of Idolatry," I.1, is the cause and root of idolatry. Aristotle, then, in his own right nearly reached the level of prophecy; he is "chief" of the philosophers who attained to such an understanding of the universe on their own steam that they rejected astrology because it leads to idolatry. Put simply, Maimonides thought very highly of Aristotle.

But not so highly that he thought that Aristotle could not err on matters of physics and metaphysics: it is well-known that Maimonides at least claimed to reject Aristotle's assertion that the universe was uncreated. It was Maimonides' argument that Aristotle was wrong on his own terms: in thinking that he could prove the eternity of the universe, Aristotle was simply doing Aristotelian philosophy poorly.[24]

But Aristotle could err in other areas as well:

> Everything that Aristotle has said about all that exists from beneath the
> sphere of the moon to the center of the earth is indubitably correct, and no
> one will deviate from it unless he does not understand it or unless he has
> preconceived opinions that he wishes to defend or that lead him to a denial
> of a thing that is manifest. On the other hand, everything that Aristotle ex-
> pounds with regard to the sphere of the moon and that which is above it is,
> except for certain things, something analogous to guessing and conjectur-
> ing. All the more does this apply to what he says about the order of the in-
> tellects and to some of the opinions regarding the divine that he believes;
> for the latter contain grave incongruities and perversities that manifestly
> and clearly appear as such to all the nations, that propagate evil, and that he
> cannot demonstrate. (II.22, pp. 319–20)

Maimonides emphasizes this point by repeating it:

> I shall repeat here what I have said before [II.22]. All that Aristotle states
> about that which is beneath the sphere of the moon is in accordance with
> reasoning; these are things that have a known cause, that follow one upon
> the other, and concerning which it is clear and manifest at what points wis-
> dom and natural providence are effective. However, regarding all that is in
> the heavens, man grasps nothing but a small measure of what is mathe-
> matical; and you know what is in it. (II.24, p. 326)

Why was Aristotle mistaken in this fashion? Maimonides explains: "However,
as I have let you know, the science of astronomy was not in his [Aristotle's]
time what it is today" (II.19, p. 308).[25] The mathematical sciences, while not
perfected in Aristotle's time, had ultimately reached or at least come close to
perfection; Aristotle had brought the physics of the sublunar world to perfection and closure;[26] Galen had brought anatomy to a state of great perfection.

With respect to the ever greater approximation of truth in the various
spheres of philosophy (what we would call "science" today), we just saw that
Maimonides held that the mathematical sciences were incorrectly understood in Aristotle's day; in his own day they had reached a much higher level
of perfection. This is true not only of the mathematical sciences, but also of
anatomy: "[Galen] attained enormous success in anatomy, and things became
clear to him in his time that were not apparent to anyone else. In addition,
the activities and functions of organs, and their physiology, as well as conditions of the pulse which were not clear at the time of Aristotle [were understood and explained by Galen]."[27] Finally, with respect to astronomical
matters, Maimonides thought that his own knowledge might be superseded:
"It is possible that someone else will find a demonstration by means of which

the true reality of what is obscure for me will become clear to him" (*Guide of the Preplexed* II.24, p. 327). Without getting into the vexed question of when the idea of progress entered Western culture, we can see here that Maimonides admitted the fact of scientific development and even anticipated that science would develop beyond what he himself, or, more accurately, what his generation, had been able to accomplish in it.[28]

Maimonides thought very highly of Aristotle, so highly that he placed him on the scale of human excellence just beneath the prophets. But science had progressed since Aristotle's day, and human beings living in Maimonides' era (close to fifteen hundred years after Aristotle) knew much more than did the Stagirite. There is no decline of the generations here! Can it be seriously thought that Maimonides would hold that secular scientists have progressed while "Jewish scientists," so to speak, have regressed?[29]

IV. Spiritual Progress

In terms of what we can call "spiritual progress," Maimonides indicates that human beings grow and develop from generation to generation, both as individuals and as a race.[30] As individuals, Maimonides maintained in one of the most notorious passages in the *Guide of the Perplexed*, the generation of the Exodus was unable to worship God in a truly mature fashion and needed a sacrificial cult:

> For a sudden transition from one opposite to another is impossible. And therefore man, according to his nature, is not capable of abandoning suddenly all to which he was accustomed . . . and as at that time the way of life generally accepted and customary in the whole world and the universal service upon which we were brought up consisted in offering various species of living beings in the temples. . . . His wisdom, may He be exalted, and His gracious ruse, which is manifest in regard to all His creatures did not require that He give us a Law prescribing the rejection, abandonment, and abolition of all these kinds of worship. . . . At that time this would have been similar to the appearance of a prophet in these times who, calling upon the people to worship God, would say: "God has given you a Law forbidding you to pray to Him, to fast, to call upon Him for help in misfortune. Your worship should consist solely in meditation without any works at all." Therefore He, may He be exalted, suffered the above-mentioned kinds of worship to remain" (III.32, p. 526).[31]

Our forefathers may have been religious primitives; spiritual development had taken place since the days of the Exodus, however, and some Jews in Maimonides' day were ready to be told how to worship God truly. In III.51,

Maimonides explains that in order to achieve true worship we must first strengthen the bond of intellect between ourselves and God. Having attained that apprehension, we can then truly love God ("love is proportionate to apprehension"). After love of God, comes true worship: it consists in setting thought to work on the first intelligible and to devoting oneself exclusively to this as far as this is within one's capacity." (p. 621)

Individual human beings have developed spiritually to the point where they can truly worship God through intellectual meditation.[32] Eventually, as we have seen in our discussion of messianism, Maimonides holds that all human beings will reach the point where the devote themselves to nothing but the knowledge of the Lord. Here, too, we see that Maimonides expects humanity to achieve ever greater levels of spirituality, not the reverse.

V. Semikhah and Later Courts

Maimonides' comments on two rather technical issues, the possibility of the reintroduction of *semikhah*, the formal ordination of judges, and the authority of later courts vis-à-vis earlier ones, also clearly indicate his understanding that later generations can be superior to earlier ones.[33]

M. Sanhedrin I.3 reads: "The laying on of the elder's hands and the breaking of the heifer's neck require the presence of three judges . . ." On this Maimonides writes:

"The laying on of the elder's hands" refers to the ordination of judges. . . . "There is no ordination outside of the land of Israel."[34] Both the one to be ordained and those conferring the ordination upon him must be in the land of Israel. . . . I believe that if all the disciples and Rabbis were to agree to appoint one man over the Yeshiva, that is to make him the head of the Yeshiva—provided this took place in the land of Israel as aforementioned—that man in fact becomes the leader of the Yeshiva and is ordained and can then himself ordain anyone else he chooses. For if you do not follow this principle it would be impossible ever to have the Great Court, because each member of that court would have to ordained and without a doubt. Indeed, God long ago promised us their return, as it is written, *And I will restore thy judges as at the first* (Isa. 1:26). If you believe that the Messiah will appoint them even though they are not ordained—this is to be denied, because we have already explained at the beginning of this composition of ours that the Messiah will not add to the Torah nor delete from it, not the written Torah, nor the oral Torah. I believe that the Sanhedrin will be restored before the coming of the Messiah and that this will be one of the signs of his coming, as it is written, *And I will restore thy judges as at the first and thy counselors as at the beginning; afterward thou shalt be called the city of righteousness* (Isa. 1:26).

> This will undoubtedly occur when God will prepare the hearts of human beings so that their good works increase and their longing for God and His Torah increase and their righteousness increases. All this will precede the coming of the Messiah, as is explained in many scriptural passages.[35]

We learn a number of important things from this passage. For our purposes the most important is that *semikhah* can be reinstituted without divine or messianic intervention (in fact, *semikhah* must be reinstituted by human efforts in order to make possible the coming of the Messiah). With the re-introduction of ordination, the reconstitution of the great court, the *Sanhedrin*, becomes possible. In terms of formal authority, a properly constituted *Sanhedrin* is vastly superior to any earlier court whose members were not ordained. Here we see that Maimonides had no problems with the idea that later (pre-messianic) courts could have greater authority than earlier courts, hardly the position we would expect an exponent of the decline of the generations to adopt.

This point becomes clearer when we examine Maimonides' explicit comments on the relative authority of earlier and later courts. Mishnah Eduyot I:5 reads: ". . . no court may set aside the decision of another court unless it is greater than [the first] in number and wisdom . . . " In his commentary on this text, Maimonides writes,

> The intent of this halakhah is that if a court acted according to the opinion of an individual, another court cannot dispute it [i.e., the first court] for that reason, and establish the law according the opinion of the majority, unless its number were greater than that of the earlier court which acted according to that individual, and wiser than it, i.e., that the head [lit.: head of the yeshiva] of this court was wiser than that of the earlier one.

Maimonides' comment here should be read in conjunction with another passage in his writings, *Mishneh Torah*, "Laws of the Rebellious Elder," II.1–3:

> [1] If the Great Court, by employing one of the hermeneutical principles, deduced a ruling which in its judgment was in consonance with the law and rendered a decision to that effect, and a later court finds a reason for setting aside a ruling, it may do so and act in accordance with its own opinion . . .
> [2] If a court instituted a decree, enacted an ordinance, or introduced a custom, which was universally accepted in Israel, and a later court wishes to rescind the measure, to abolish the ordinance, decree, or custom, it is not empowered to do so, unless it is superior to the former both in point of wisdom and in point of number. If it is superior in wisdom, but not in number, or in number, but not in wisdom, it is denied the right to abrogate the measure adopted by its predecessor, even if the reason which prompted the latter to enact the decree or ordinance has lost all force. But how is it possible

for any court to exceed another in number, seeing that each consists of seventy-one members? We include in the number the Rabbis of the age, who agree to accept without demur the decision of the [contemporaneous] court. [3] The last ruling applies only to prohibitive measures, which, like many other measures, do not have as their purpose the safeguarding of the Torah. But decrees and prohibitions designed by the court to serve as a protective fence [around the Torah], if they have been universally accepted in Israel, no later great court, even if it be superior to the former, is empowered to abrogate or permit.

In these two texts Maimonides clearly allows for the possibility that later courts can be greater in number *and in wisdom* than earlier courts.[36] His decision here is on particular interest in light of the Talmud's assumption that such can never be the case.[37]

In understanding Maimonides in this fashion I follow R. Joseph Karo in his *Kesef Mishneh* ad loc. Karo asks if a later court could indeed set aside the decisions of an earlier court, why the Amoraim never disputed the positions of Tannaim? As Karo understands Maimonides, the latter obviously held that Amoraim had the right [*reshut*] to dispute the Tannaim. "It is possible to say," he writes, seeking to understand Maimonides' reasoning, "that from the day of the completion [lit. sealing] of the Mishnah it was established and accepted that later generations [Amoraim] would not dispute the earlier generations [Tannaim]; so also did they do with the completion [lit. sealing] of the Gemara, [agreeing] that from the day of its completion, no man had the right to dispute it." This is, indeed, Maimonides' position as expressed in the Introduction to the *Mishneh Torah*. Amoraim were not themselves necessarily innately inferior to Tannaim; that they refused to dispute Tannaim reflects a decision *accepted*, not an objective situation in effect *imposed* upon them because of their inferiority. As we have seen earlier, Karo himself accepts the doctrine of the decline of the generations. From his discussion here it seems obvious that he realized that Maimonides did not accept the doctrine, a fact which Karo seems to accept with equanimity.

Maimonides did not assume that each generation or each age was necessarily inferior to its predecessors. On the contrary, his view of history seemed to involve the idea of development upward, not downward. This development may be punctuated by periods of backsliding (as we have seen, he thought that he was living in such a period) but the overall thrust continues: onward and upward, towards the messianic era. This being the case, why indeed do the Tannaim and Amoraim enjoy the authority they undoubtedly enjoy, at least in strictly and technically halakhic matters? To this issue we turn in the next chapter.

CHAPTER 6

On the Nature
of the Rabbis' Authority

To this point, we have been concerned to show that Maimonides denies the doctrine of the decline of the generations; that he rejects the related claim that the Tannaim and Amoraim were inherently superior to all subsequent generations of Jews; that he affirms that the Tannaim and Amoraim could and did err on scientific matters; and that their (non-halakhic) exegesis of Biblical verses was not normative for later generations of Jews. In brief, Maimonides held that the Rabbis were human beings essentially like all other human beings. This being the case, why are subsequent generations of Jews barred from disputing the Rabbis' halakhic positions and decisions?

Maimonides' answer to this question is fairly straightforward: through a combination of personal piety, devotion to Torah, and philosophical acumen (all of a high but decidedly not supernatural degree), combined with a particular historical circumstance, the authors of the Mishnah and Talmud had achieved a level of formal authority within the Jewish community never since duplicated. That this authority was a function of the role played by the Rabbis in Jewish history, and not a function of their own innate greatness (not that Maimonides sought to belittle their qualities), in no way diminishes it.

I. The Introduction to the *Mishneh Torah*

Maimonides' clearest statement of his position is in his Introduction to the *Mishneh Torah*.[1] This is a long text, and I will present portions of it here (in Hyamson's translation), interpolating my commentary on it. Maimonides opens with a history of the transmission of the Oral Torah to the time of R. Judah the Prince, in the tradition called simply "Rabbi" and referred to by Maimonides as "our holy teacher." He then continues:

> Our holy teacher compiled the Mishnah. From the time of Moses our Master to that of our holy teacher, no work had been composed from which the Oral Torah had been publicly taught . . . [R. Judah] gathered together all the traditions, enactments, interpretations, and expositions of every portion of the Torah, that had either come down from Moses, our Master, or had been deduced by the courts in successive generations. All this material he redacted in the Mishnah, which was diligently taught in public, and thus became universally known among the Jewish people. Copies of it were made and widely disseminated, so that the Oral Torah might not be forgotten in Israel.

The Mishnah of R. Judah the Prince was comprehensive and universally known to (and, it is important to add, accepted by) the Jewish people. In these two characteristics, it was similar to the Torah of Moses. R. Judah, it should be understood, made every effort to see to that this text was widely disseminated and accepted. Maimonides continues:

> Why did our holy teacher act so and not leave things as they were? Because he observed that the number of disciples was diminishing, fresh calamities were continually happening, the wicked Government was extending its domain and increasing in power, and Israelites were wandering and emigrating to distant countries. He therefore composed a work to serve as a handbook for all, and the contents of which could be rapidly studied and would not be forgotten. Throughout his life, he and his colleagues were engaged in giving public instruction in the Mishnah.

What led R. Judah to compile the Mishnah? Maimonides offers a number of reasons: (a) fewer and fewer people were devoting themselves to the study of Torah; perhaps because (b) the Jews were being overcome by fresh calamities; and, (c) the Roman Empire was extending its area of sovereignty and its power; in consequence, no doubt, of the last two points, and certainly contributing to the first, the Jews were leaving the Land of Israel. As a result of all this, R. Judah composed a summary of the Oral Torah, one which could be rapidly studied and would not easily be forgotten. He and his colleagues then devoted themselves to teaching the Mishnah publicly.

Maimonides' account of the redaction of the Babylonian Talmud paints a similar picture:

> Ravina and Rav Ashi and their colleagues were the last of the great sages who firmly established the Oral Torah, made decrees, and ordinances, and introduced customs. Their decrees, ordinances, and customs obtained universal acceptance among Israelites wherever they settled. After the court of Rav Ashi, who compiled the Gemara which was finally completed in the days of

his son, an extraordinarily great dispersion of Israel throughout the world took place. The people emigrated to remote parts and distant isles. The prevalence of wars and the march of armies made travel insecure. The study of the Torah declined. The Jewish people did not flock to the colleges in their thousands and tens of thousands as heretofore; but in each city and country, individuals who felt the divine call gathered together and occupied themselves with the Torah, studied all the works of the sages, and from these, learned the method of legal interpretation.[2]

The "decrees, ordinances, and customs" of the redactors of the Babylonian Talmud, Ravina and Rav Ashi, "obtained universal acceptance among Israelites wherever they settled." They were the last Jewish leaders to enjoy this success. *After* the close of the Talmud "extraordinarily great dispersion of Israel throughout the world took place." The Talmud was not edited because of this dispersion; rather, this dispersion guaranteed that no subsequent compilation of Jewish law would achieve the level of authority of the Talmud. As was true of the time of the Mishnah, the political situation rendered life insecure; the Jewish people were dispersing, and fewer and fewer were devoting themselves to Torah. The study of the Torah became a matter of groups of individuals, not the inheritance of the people as a whole. In consequence of this,

> If a court established in any country, after the time of the Talmud, made decrees and ordinances or introduced customs for those residing in its particular country, or for the residents of other countries, its enactments did not obtain the acceptance of all Israel because of the remoteness of Jewish settlements and difficulties of travel.

Post-Talmudic courts, due to the unfortunate historical fact of the great dispersion of Israel, have authority only over the areas of their immediate jurisdiction. Put more accurately, the jurisdiction of post-Talmudic courts is limited to the areas in which they reside and over which they in fact hold sway. This is not the place to go into the jurisprudential question of how Maimonides understands a court's authority to be determined, but it is clear from this text that at least in part a court has de jure authority only to the extent that it has de facto authority. Be that as it may, the difference between the Talmudic and post-Talmudic periods, and the authority of Rabbis in each period to make decrees and ordinances or introduce customs, relates to the concentration or dispersion of the Jews. The Talmud is universally authoritative because it was universally accepted; no post-Talmudic compilation has achieved that degree of acceptance and hence no post-Talmudic compilation has achieved that level of authority.[3]

Maimonides expands on this point, comparing post-Talmudic courts to the Sanhedrin. The latter, it appears from his discussion, represented all

Israel, while the former are composed of individuals who represent, at most, themselves, as it were, and those of their immediate compatriots who know and accept their authority:

> And as the court of any particular country consisted of individuals [only] while the Great Court of Seventy had, several years before the compilation of the Talmud ceased to exist,[4] no compulsion is exercised on those living in one country to observe the customs of another country; nor is any court directed to issue a decree that had been issued by another court in the same country.

Thus, Jews living in country B are not compelled to accept the decisions of courts in country A; even in the same country, different courts do not have to accept each other's authority.

The distinction between the authority of the Talmud and post-Talmudic courts is crucial:

> So too, if one of the Geonim taught that a certain way of judgment was correct, and it became clear to a court at a later date that this was not in accordance with the view of the Gemara, the earlier authority is not necessarily followed but that view is adopted which seems more reasonable, whether it be that of an earlier or later authority. The foregoing observations refer to rules, decrees, ordinances, and customs that originated after the Talmud had been compiled.

After the close of the Talmud every authority is by definition a local authority. The authority of courts and decisors after the close of the Talmud is radically restricted compared to that of the Talmud itself:

> But whatever is already mentioned in the Babylonian Talmud is binding on all Israel. And every city and country is bound to observe all the customs observed by the sages of the Gemara, promulgate their decrees, and uphold their institutions.

What is the reason for this dramatic difference? Let the reader recall that for Rav Sherira Gaon the diminished authority of post-Talmudic rabbis is a consequence of their being personally inferior to the Rabbis of the Talmud. Maimonides, however, explains that the "Babylonian Talmud is binding on all Israel. . . . "

> on the grounds that all these customs, decrees, and institutions mentioned in the Talmud received the assent of all Israel, and those sages who instituted the ordinances, issued the decrees, introduced the customs, gave the

decisions and taught that a certain ruling was correct, constituted the total body or the majority of the sages of Israel. They were the leaders who received from each other the traditions concerning the fundamentals of Judaism, in unbroken succession back to Moses, our Master, peace upon him.

This text is crucial for our purposes. The authority of the Talmud derives from (a) its having received "the assent of all Israel"; (b) the fact that its Rabbis "constituted the total body or the majority of the sages of Israel"; and (c) the chain of transmission to them from Moses was unbroken. The objective historical fact of dispersion and the dislocations caused by it and the persecutions associated with it, meant that the Talmud was the last Jewish text to satisfy these three criteria. Maimonides makes this point graphically and tragically clear in the sequel:

> In our days, severe vicissitudes prevail, and all feel the pressure of hard times. The wisdom of our wise men has disappeared, the understanding of our prudent men is hidden.

Maimonides spells the situation out in great detail:

> Hence the commentaries of the Geonim and their compilations of laws and responses, which they took care to make clear, have in our times become hard to understand so that only a few individuals properly comprehend them. Needless to add that such is the case in regard to the Talmud itself— the Babylonian as well as the Palestinian—the *Sifra*, the *Sifri*, and the *Tosefta*, all of which works require, for their comprehension, a broad mind, a wise soul and considerable study, and then one can learn from them the correct practice as to what is forbidden or permitted, and the other rules of the Torah.

Texts which at one time were clear and easily understood have become nearly incomprehensible, not because people are less intelligent than they used to be, but because of "severe vicissitudes" and the "pressure of hard times."

This situation is the background to Maimonides' decision to write the *Mishneh Torah*:

> On these grounds I, Moses the son of Maimon of Spain, bestirred myself and, relying upon the help of God, blessed be He, intently studied all these works, with the view of putting together the results obtained from them in regard to what is forbidden or permitted, clean or unclean, and the other rules of the Torah—all in plain language and terse style so that thus the entire Oral Torah might become systematically known to all, without citing difficulties and solutions, or differences of view, one person saying so, and another

something else,—but consisting of statements, clear and convincing, and in accordance with the conclusions drawn from all these compilations and commentaries that have appeared from the time of Moses to the present, so that all the rules shall be accessible to young and old, whether these appertain to the [biblical] commandments or to the institutions established by the sages and prophets, so that no other work should be needed for ascertaining any of the laws of Israel, but that this work might serve as a compendium of the entire Oral Torah, including the ordinances, customs, and decrees instituted from the days of our Moses our master till the compilation of the Talmud, as expounded for us by the Geonim in all the works composed by them since the completion of the Talmud.

Clearly following the example of "our holy teacher," R. Judah the Prince, Maimonides, the second Moses, sought to make "the entire Oral Torah . . . systematically known to all." In order to do so he compiled a comprehensive, apodictic "compendium of the entire Oral Torah." No shrinking violet, Maimonides gave his work a name appropriate to its content and aim:

Hence I have entitled this work *Mishneh Torah* ["Repetition of the Torah"], for the reason that a person, who first reads the Written Torah and then this compilation, will know from it the whole of the Oral Torah, without having to consult any book between them.

Not surprisingly, this text aroused the amazement and ire of generations of Maimonides' commentators and much ink has been spilt to prove that Maimonides did not mean that Jews should cease studying those texts compiled between the canonization of the Torah and the publication of the *Mishneh Torah*. That point, however, is not strictly relevant to our concerns here.[5]

Returning to the issue at hand, we see in this long text how Maimonides explains the authority of the Talmud *vis-à-vis* later texts. Where Rav Sherira grounds the superior authority of the Talmud (and within the Talmud the authority of the Mishnah over the Gemara) on the decline of the generations, Maimonides all but ignores the distinction between Mishnah and Gemara and understands the superior authority of the Talmud in what can only be called historically contingent terms: the Talmud is the last halakhic text to enjoy the assent of all Israel and be promulgated by the Rabbis as a cohesive body, who were part of an unbroken chain of tradition stretching back to Moses. The authority of the Rabbis of the Talmud by and large has nothing to do with their personal qualities (not that Maimonides would want to express anything but the highest regard for those qualities) and everything to do with the fact that they satisfy certain formal criteria.[6]

II. Semikhah

My interpretation of Maimonides' Introduction to the *Mishneh Torah* may be supported by looking once again at Maimonides' attitude towards the reintroduction of rabbinic ordination.[7] Ordination (*semikhah*) was required of members of the Sanhedrin and of judges in a variety of kinds of cases. Maimonides ("Laws of the Sanhedrin," IV.1), traces ordination back to Moses in an uninterrupted chain. It may be conferred only in the Land of Israel (IV.6). It is an accepted element of traditional Jewish self-understanding that at some point the chain of Mosaic ordination was interrupted. This is generally thought to have happened during the fifth century.

Maimonides deals with the reintroduction of ordination in two places. As we saw in the last chapter, M. Sanhedrin I.3 ordains: "The laying on of the elder's hands and the breaking of the heifer's neck require the presence of three judges . . . " On this, as we have seen, Maimonides comments:

> "The laying on of the elder's hands" refers to the ordination of judges. . . .
> "There is no ordination outside of the land of Israel." Both the one to be or-
> dained and those conferring the ordination upon him must be in the land
> of Israel. . . . I believe that if all[8] the disciples and Rabbis were to agree to ap-
> point one man over the Yeshiva, that is to make him the head of the
> Yeshiva—provided this took place in the land of Israel as aforementioned—
> that man in fact becomes the leader of the Yeshiva and is ordained and can
> then himself ordain anyone else he chooses. For if you do not follow this
> principle it would be impossible ever to have the Great Court, because each
> member of that court would have to ordained and without a doubt. . . . [9]

Renewal of ordination, then, requires that "all" (i.e., most) of the rabbis of the land of Israel[10] agree to ordain one of their number. This must be the case, argues Maimonides, for otherwise the Sanhedrin could never be reconstituted. Reconstitution of the Sanhedrin, he goes on to argue in the sequel to this passage, must take place before the coming of the Messiah and is, indeed, one of the signs of his imminent coming. This being the case, if ordination could not be reinstated, the Messiah could never come!

Maimonides returns to this issue in the *Mishneh Torah*. "Laws of the Sanhedrin," IV.11 reads in part:

> . . . It seems to me that if all the Sages [*hakhamim*] in the land of Israel
> [even though none of them are ordained] were to agree to appoint judges
> and to ordain them, the ordination would be valid, empowering the or-
> dained to adjudicate cases involving fines[11] and to ordain others. If what we
> have said is true, the question arises: Why were the Sages concerned over

[the abolition of] ordination, apprehensive that the laws concerning fines might be abolished [so much so that R. Judah ben Baba (Sanh 14a) martyred himself in order to ordain others]? Because Israel is scattered and agreement on the part of all is impossible.

Here again the crucial issue is the dispersion of Israel and assent by all (i.e., most) of the Rabbis to the act of ordination. Could these historically conditioned factors be overcome, ordination could be renewed.

For our purposes, the importance of these texts lies in the explicit emphasis on concerted, unified action on the part of the Rabbis of the Land of Israel. Such an effort could reinstitute ordination; the reinstitution of ordination would allow for the recreation of the Sanhedrin; the recreation of the Sanhedrin, it appears, would allow for the revision of Talmudic law. The authority of the rabbis of the Talmud, then, is not a function of their own, inherent and unduplicatable qualities, but a function of the role they played in history, a role which can be played again if historical circumstances permit.[12]

The Introduction to the *Mishneh Torah* shows clearly that for Maimonides the Tannaim and Amoraim have authority to determine matters of Halakhah greater than any later convocation of rabbis. This authority, however, has nothing to do with the innate character of the Rabbis, everything to do with the special historical circumstances in which the Rabbis found themselves. Later generations of rabbis would have the same authority when the Sanhedrin was reconstituted.

CHAPTER 7

Concluding
(Quasi-) Scientific Postscript

I think that it is likely that some readers of this book may come away with a sense of disappointment. Readers of Maimonides, the philosopher, who approach his works primarily from the vantage point of the *Guide of the Perplexed*, might think the work trivial: I have proved that for Maimonides the Tannaim and Amoraim are human beings like all others with respect to their native intellectual and spiritual capacities. One must accept their halakhic determinations, but with respect to all other matters one is free to weigh, measure, consider, accept, reject, or modify their opinions. Their halakhic authority is a consequence of historical circumstance, not their innate capacities. Last, human capacities have not been declining since the time of the Rabbis; if anything, we can expect them to grow, not decline. The reader of Maimonides the philosopher may ask, "So what else is new? Could any careful reader of Maimonides, the student of Aristotle and al-Farabi, really believe that he attributed super-human capabilities to the Rabbis, accepted their authority on scientific matters blindly, or accepted some notion of the decline of the generations?"

Many students of the Rambam, author of the *Mishneh Torah* and other seminal works of rabbinics, on the other hand, are likely to reject the conclusions of this study as prima facie ridiculous, unworthy of serious refutation. How is it possible, the might ask, to take seriously the idea that Maimonides put himself as far out of the rabbinic mainstream as he is presented as doing in this book?

The interpretation of Maimonides presented here, however, is neither trivial nor ridiculous; it is true, and significantly so, since it once again illustrates the essential unity of Maimonides' thought. Many readers of Maimonides approach him as if he belonged primarily to a tradition opening with Plato and Aristotle and continuing through Hellenistic philosophers like Alexander of Aphrodisias and Themistius, and Muslim thinkers like ibn Sina and al-Farabi, continuing on through Maimonides himself to Aquinas, Spinoza, and Kant.[1] Other readers of Maimonides picture him as belonging exclusively to a tradition which opens with the first Moses, through the prophets, Tannaim, Amoraim, Geonim, and through Maimonides himself to the Rishonim and Aharonim. Maimonides, however, actually lived at the intersection of these two vectors; presenting in the light of only one or the other is radically to misrepresent him.

I have written here what I hope is a convincing work of scholarship. But, given Maimonides' stature, and the use to which he is put in contemporary Judaism, few if any works of scholarship on him can really be divorced from the life of the scholar writing about him. This is all more the case if the scholar in question (myself) is an observant Jew living in Israel. This study has certain implications for contemporary Judaism and fairness to the reader demands that I make them and my personal standpoint clear, to the greatest extent that I can. In so doing, I will also summarize my arguments and conclusions, pulling them together for the reader, but not in the order in which they are presented above; rather, I shall present these matters in the order in which I came to understand them.

It will be useful to begin with how I came to write this book. Several years ago I heard a lecture in which the speaker, a well-known scientist affiliated with the Habad movement, affirmed that since Maimonides wrote the *Mishneh Torah* with divine inspiration, we must take very word in it as correct and authoritative, including the Ptolemaic description of the universe presented in the first four chapters of "Laws of the Foundations of the Torah."

This piqued my interest. "This may be the Habad view of Maimonides," I thought, "but is it Maimonides' view of Maimonides?" I examined the issue and wrote an essay seeking to prove that Maimonides made no Habad-like claims about the authority of his own work.[2] Among other things, I showed that Maimonides occasionally rejected the scientific teachings of the Rabbis and argued that he could hardly have held his own science to be more authoritative than theirs.[3] At this point I understood that Maimonides clearly distinguished the authority of the Rabbis in halakhic matters from their authority in other fields, but I did not realize that there was much more to the story than that.

Traditionalist Jews today strongly affirm the notion of the "decline of the generations" as a matter of fundamental dogma. This hyper-conservatism may be understood as a reaction to the challenges of modernity in general and of Conservative Judaism in particular. Conservative Judaism is understood in the Orthodox world as teaching that contemporary rabbis have as much authority as the Tannaim and Amoraim to make Halakhah; in effect, to participate as equals in what they see as the ongoing creation of Judaism. One

effective way of arguing against such a position is to affirm that the Rabbis of
the Mishnah and Talmud enjoy unchallengeable authority because of who
they were as individuals—individuals innately superior to all subsequent
generations. If the Rabbis were angels, and we are asses, then how can we
have the hutzpah to arrogate to ourselves the right to question them, con-
trovert them, or "adjust" their teachings to "new" realities?

Such is the power of accepted ways of thinking, that having been raised
as an Orthodox Jew, and living happily as one to this day, it never occurred to
me until I thought about it in the context of this study, that Maimonides
might not accept this picture of the authority of the Rabbis. Such is the power
of habit and upbringing furthermore, as Maimonides himself often complains, that even though I was familiar with Maimonides' Introduction to the
Mishneh Torah (analyzed in the previous chapter), and even though I had
read Isadore Twersky's studies of it, I had never consciously realized that Maimonides affirmed the formal, "constitutional" authority of the Rabbis without attributing to them any superhuman capabilities. From Maimonides'
perspective, Conservative Judaism (as it is understood by contemporary Orthodoxy, at least) is wrong (the Rabbis of the Mishnah and Talmud do have a
kind of constitutive authority unmatched by any other pre-messianic group
of rabbis) and so is Orthodoxy (the authority of the Rabbis has nothing to do
with their innate qualities: they are normal human beings, and so are we).

After thinking about it, I realized that Maimonides could not have held
any other position: his theory of nature and miracles (discussed above in
chapter 2) disallowed it. Human nature is stable and there is no way that he
could account for the sort of changes in human nature posited by the idea of
the "decline of the generations." That being the case, whatever authority the
Rabbis had must derive from the *role* they played in Jewish life and history,
not from their unduplicatable qualities: from *who* they were, in other words,
not from *what* they were.

I was then forced to ask myself, was Maimonides' position on the "decline of the generations" as revolutionary in his day as it appears to Orthodox
Jews today? My negative answer to that question is explained and defended in
chapter 1 above. The Talmud clearly preserves texts *out of which* a theory of
intellectual and spiritual decline was derived without itself teaching such a
theory, or even being informed generally by such ideas. Later generations of
Jewish leaders (Rav Sherira in his battle against the Karaites, Hakham Nieto
in his polemics with "Protestant" tendencies introduced into seventeenth
century Judaism, and contemporary Orthodox rabbis in their battles against
the forces of reform in Judaism[4]), read the theory *into* the Talmud. Upon in-
spection, it simply turns out that there is no reason in the world to think that
Maimonides understood the Rabbis to hold such a doctrine or (were he able

to express himself in such terms) that he thought that their world view was informed by it.

In other words, Maimonides adopts revolutionary, seemingly heterodox positions, on many topics. It is my understanding, however, that in his ignoring the notion of the decline of the generations, and in his understanding of the formal nature of rabbinic authority, he was not staking out new or unprecedented positions. This claim would, no doubt, surprise most traditionalist Jews today, but it is supported by the facts as marshalled in chapter 1 of this study.

Having reached this point in the examination of the issues, I was forced to confront the many passages in which Maimonides deplores the degenerate nature of his times. Might not these complaints be an expression of his acceptance of the notion of the decline of the generations? My analysis of these texts is presented above in chapter 3: what ever may be the problems with the time in which he lived, these problems were the consequences of objective historical and social factors, not some immanent process of decline in the Jewish people.

Maimonides, it thus turns out, could not have affirmed that human nature was in some sort of constant process of entropic decline, and, in fact, did not. He thus refused to affirm that the Rabbis of the Mishnah and Talmud were significantly different in their natures from the rabbis of his day (or, it is fair to add, ours). From this there followed an attitude of freedom towards the teachings of these Rabbis which would be considered scandalous in traditionalist Jewish circles today (and, it is fair to add, was so considered by many of Maimonides' own contemporaries as well).

Not only did Maimonides not affirm a doctrine of decline, but examination of his teachings concerning the Messiah, prayer, scientific "progress," and the authority of courts of law, shows that he actually held an opposed view, that later generations could (and would) accomplish more than earlier generations, thanks to their own attainments, and not just because they stood "on the shoulders of giants." These issues are taken up in chapter 5 above.

I do not want what I have written in chapter 5 to be misunderstood; I shall thus digress here for a moment, to take note of the implications of Maimonides' messianic teachings and the uses to which they are put in the Jewish world today, especially in Israel. Maimonides affirms a kind of messianic naturalism which makes possible the claim that human beings can contribute to the coming of the Messiah. Whether or not this was Maimonides' own position is irrelevant here; it is certainly a possible implication of his stance. Orthodox Zionists of various stripes use Maimonides to bolster their arguments against ultra-Orthodox non- or anti-Zionists, who by and large minimize the value of practical, this-worldly contributions to the coming of the Messiah.

Maimonides' messianism figures in a second contemporary debate, this one within the Orthodox Zionist camp itself. Some of these individuals argue that a good "maimonidean" Zionist must work for the coming of the Messiah; a major aspect of the Messiah's work is the settling of the Jews in and upon the Land of Israel, as the latter was defined in the Torah; giving up portions of that territory is tantamount to retarding the coming the Messiah. Other Orthodox Zionists (such as myself) argue that a good "maimonidean" Zionist must work for the coming of the Messiah; a major aspect of the Messiah's work is the institution of just peace in the world as a whole and the Land of Israel most particularly; adopting policies which oppose peace is tantamount to retarding the coming of the Messiah.

Maimonides' messianism is this-worldly and thus lends itself to the sorts of uses described here. It is this aspect of his teachings which made them so attractive to Habad. Wanting to ground an immanent/imminent messianism in classic texts,[5] they found Maimonides a convenient hook on which to hang their messianic enthusiasm. My own feeling, for whatever it is worth, is that Habad had to push Maimonides' texts pretty hard to make them refer to the Lubavitcher Rebbe, but as Maimonides himself once remarked, "the gates of interpretation are never sealed."

Hawkish and dovish Orthodox Zionists on the one hand, and Lubavitcher Hassidim on the other, however, tend to obscure the fact that for Maimonides the whole point of the Messiah's coming is to make it possible for humans to achieve the sort of perfection which is a prerequisite for earning a share in the (transcendent) world to come. His immanentism serves transcendentalism and this ought never be forgotten.

Returning to the theme of our study, if the Rabbis are human beings like Maimonides (and the readers of these words), and if they have no special innate qualities which confer upon them a species of intellectual and spiritual authority which makes disagreeing with them heretical (a kind of doctrine of "Rabbinic infallibility"), and if Maimonides did in fact disagree with their pronouncements in many areas, and if human beings can be expected to grow, and progress, and become better, then why is it that Maimonides accords to the Tannaim and Amoraim the authority to determine Halakhah, an authority he gives no subsequent (pre-Messianic) generation? This is the subject taken up in chapter 6 of this book. It was shown there that it is Maimonides' doctrine that the Rabbis have what may be called a kind of "constitutive halakhic authority" because they satisfied objective historical criteria. Were other groups of rabbis to satisfy these criteria, they would have the same authority. Indeed, it appears to be Maimonides' position that with the coming the Messiah such will precisely be the case.

Maimonides' position as sketched out in this book preserves rabbinic authority without sacrificing the intellectual freedom needed to search for truth in all fields and in all ages. In so doing it reflects Maimonides' conviction that Torah and science ("wisdom"—*hokhmah* in Maimonides' own terminology) must go hand in hand, and further reflects the way his science (concerning the "nature of nature") underlay his Torah.

Notes

Preface

1. I have found Robert Nisbet, *History of the Idea of Progress* (New York: Basic Books, 1980) to be a very useful introduction to this whole subject. See in particular, pp. 151–56. Further on the medieval "quarrel" see the symposium in *The Journal of the History of Ideas* 48 (1987): 3–50; and Albert Zimmermann (ed.), *Antiqui und Moderni* (*=Miscellanea Mediaevalia* 9) (Berlin: Walter de Gruyter, 1974).

Introduction

1. Michael Seth Berger uses the same example in his dissertation, "The Authority of the Babylonian Talmud: Analysis of its Justification and a Proposal for a Contemporary Model," (Columbia University, 1992). This facinating dissertation reached me while I was revising the present book for publication. Berger also cites the useful distinction of R. S. Peters between being *in* authority and being *an* authority. See Peters' contribution to the symposium on "authority" in the "Aristotelian Society Supplement" 32 (1958): 207–24. I should like to take this opportunity to draw the reader's intention to Menachem Fisch's facinating discussion of different Tannaitic attitudes towards the authority of their own traditions in his forthcoming "*Qohelet* in Context—A Study of Wisdom as Constructive Skepticism," in I. C. Jarvie and N. Laor eds., *The Enterprise of Critical Rationalism* (Boston: Kluwer). In press.

2. The medical advice of the Rabbis of the Talmud (such as is found in BT Gittin, seventh chapter) is rarely followed today, it is true, but various excuses are put forward for that; in most traditionalist Jewish circles today it is not acceptable simply to say that on these medical matters the Rabbis were wrong.

3. There is a weaker claim, it must be admitted, namely, that in the area of halakhah, too, one treats the views of the Rabbis with respect but not as binding. This is not a view which one can seriously attribute to Maimonides. Similarly with the claim (suggested to me in a private communication by Menachem Fisch) that the

authority of the Rabbis in halakhic matters has nothing to do with their inherent characteristics, but with the fact that any tradition must of necessity deteriorate through time, through failures of transmission and reception. On this basis, one can affirm that former generations know more than later generations, without affirming any variant of the notion of the decline of the generations. Maimonides, however, does *not* make this claim and, for reasons that I will discuss below in chapter five, section 2, is not likely to find it acceptable.

4. That is not to say that Maimonides has an esoteric position on these matters, only that he never found it necessary to give explicit expression to his attitude on them. For excellent examples of the methodology, I will attempt to apply here, see Isadore Twersky, "Maimonides on Eretz Yisrael: Halakhic, Philosophic and Historical Perspectives," in Joel Kraemer ed., *Perspectives on Maimonides: Philosophical and Historical Studies* (Oxford: Oxford University Press, 1991) 257–90; and Abraham Melamed, "Maimonides on Man's Political Character—Needs and Obligations," in Moshe Idel, et al. eds., *Minhah le-Sarah* (Jerusalem: Magnes, 1994): 292–333 (Hebrew).

5. Again, I am not hinting at the exoteric/esoteric issue here. Many of Maimonides' explicit and "narrowly Jewish" positions were revolutionary. An excellent example of that is his attempt to foist dogmas upon Judaism. On this, see my *Dogma in Medieval Jewish Thought* (Oxford: Oxford University Presss, 1986), pp. 1–9 and my forthcoming, *Must a Jew Believe Anything?*

6. In addition to the first chapter of my book on dogma, see *Maimonides on Human Perfection* (Atlanta: Scholars Press, 1991); and *Maimonides on Judaism and the Jewish People* (Albany: SUNY Press, 1991). See further, "Reading Rambam: Approaches to the Interpretation of Maimonides," *Jewish History* 5 (1991): 73–93; and "The Beautiful Captive and Maimonides' Attitude Towards Gentiles," in Stephen D. Benin ed., *Jewish Gentile Relations Through the Ages* (Detroit: Wayne State University Press. In press).

7. See Shlomo Pines, "Translators's Introduction," in his translation of the *Guide of the Perplexed* (Chicago: University of Chicago Press, 1963), p. cxvii.

Chapter 1: The Decline of the Generations

1. Byron L. Sherwin, *In Partnership with God: Contemporary Jewish Law and Ethics* (Syracuse: Syracuse University Press, 1990), p. 1. See further, Louis Jacobs, *Holy Living: Saints and Saintliness in Judaism* (Northvale, NJ: Jason Aronson, 1990): 101–08. Jacobs notes that the claims made concerning the special spiritual powers of early Hasidic leaders were rejected by opponents of Hasidism as being "in flat contradiction to what had become virtually a dogma long before the age saw the rise of Hasidism, that the generations exhibit a progressive decline as they are distanced in time from the revelation at Sinai. According to this doctrine, later teachers are bound to be inferior to the ancients" (p. 101). For an exhaustive survey of the use of the doc-

trine in medieval halakhic texts, see H. Z. Zimmels, "The Significance of the Statement 'We are not acquainted anymore' as Echoed in Rabbinic Literature," M. M.
Kasher, N. Lamm, and L. Rosenfeld eds., *The Leo Jung Jubilee Volume* (New York: Jew-
ish Center, 1962): 223–35. For fifteenth-century Asheknaz in particular, see Yedidya
A. Dinari, *Hakhmei Ashkenaz be-Shilhei Yemi ha-Benayim* (Jerusalem: Mossad Bia-
lik, 1984), pp. 17–55. Further medieval sources are cited in Ephraim Kanarfogel, *Jew-
ish Education and Society in the High Middle Ages* (Deroit: Wayne State University
Press, 1992), pp. 171–72; and in Norman Lamm, *Torah Umadda: The Encounter of
Religious Learning and Worldly Knowledge in the Jewish Tradition* (Northale, NJ:
Jason Aronson, 1990), pp. 98–100.

2. See Berger, "The Authority of the Babylonian Talmud . . . ," p. 299. For a further example of the casual acceptance of the idea of the decline of the generations as
normative in Judaism, see Abraham M. Fuss, "The Study of Science and Philosophy
Justified by Jewish Tradition," *The Torah U-Madda Journal* 5 (1994): 101–14,
p. 101: "Normative Judaism accepts the proposition that the Ancients were figurative
giants in comparison to those who followed them."

3. For contemporary statements of the extreme version of the decline of the
generations, see Elijah Dessler, *Mikhtav Me-Eliyahu*, edited by Aryeh Carmel and
Alter Halpern, vol. 1 (Bnai Brak, 1965), pp. 75–77; Yizhak Zvi Margareten, *Sefer Tokef
ha-Talmud*, Reprint (Ofen, 1849; Brooklyn: 1983), pp. 16a–22a; Simhah Lieberman's
Introduction to his edition of Menahem Recanati's *Ta'amei ha-Mizvot* (London,
1962); and the discussion between Rabbis Isaiah Karelitz (the "Hazon Ish"), and
Elhanan Wasserman preserved in Z. Drori ed., *Sefer Kovetz Inyanim* (Bnai Brak,
1975), p. 199. Further on the Hazon Ish's views (concerning the authority of the Rab-
bis in general) see Sh. Greineman ed., *Kovez Iggerot me'et Maran Ba'al Hazon Ish*
(Bnai Brak, 1990), pp. 42–44, and 59; see further in the same volume, pt. 2, pp. 37–38.
For two exceptions to the otherwise near unanimous acceptance of the notion of the
decline of the generations, see Shalom Rosenberg's exposition of R. Abraham Isaac
Kook's ideas on the subject in *Torah u-Madda be-Hagut ha-Yehudit he-Hadashah*
(Jerusalem: Ministry of Education and Culture, 1988), pp. 11–15, and Yaakov Elman
on R. Zadok Rabinowitz of Lublin in "R. Zadok Hakohen on the History of Halakha,"
Tradition 21.4 (1983): 1–26. Further on R. Kook's views, see Jay Harris, *How Do We
Know This? Midrash and the Fragmentation of Modern Judaism* (Albany: SUNY Press,
1995), p. 334 and, in a polemical vein, Pinhas Alpert, " 'Decline of the Generations' or
Progress?!" *Gillayon* (Summer, 1974), pp. 44–48 (Hebrew).

4. For valuable studies of this issue, see Shlomo Z. Havlin, "On 'Literary Seal-
ing' as the Foundation for the Division of Halakhah into Epochs," in *Mehkarim
be-Sifrut ha-Talmudit* (Jerusalem: Israel Academy of Sciences, 1983): 148–92; and
Havlin's "Maimonides' *Mishneh Torah*—End of the Gaonic Period," *Ha-Ma'ayan* 5
(1965): 41–59 (both in Hebrew). With respect to the transition from Rishonim to
Aharonim, see Yisrael Ya'akov Yuval, "*Rishonim ve-Aharonim*, Antiqui et Moderni,"
Zion 54 (1992): 369–94 (Hebrew). Yuval, pp. 373–74, points out that Asheknazi and
Sephardi authorities differed on their approach to the identification of the Gaonate
as a distinct period, the former rejecting it as such, the latter accepting it.

5. The asses of R. Hanina b. Dosa and of R. Phinehas b. Jair are described in Hullin 7a and in Ta'anit 24a as having had exceptional understanding.

6. I cite the text as translated in Jacob Neusner, *The Talmud of the Land of Israel: A Preliminary Translation and Explanation*, vol. 25 (Chicago: University of Chicago Press, 1985); Gittin, p. 176.

7. See Shabbat 51a and Gittin 67a.

8. Who lived roughly two generations after R. Eleazar.

9. I.e., our abilities are tiny.

10. I.e., it is as hard for us to study as it is to force a peg into a wall.

11. I.e., sticking a finger into wax and pulling it out leaves one with nothing; or, a finger cannot really be pushed into hard wax, it only leaves a small depression.

12. I.e., a finger in a large pit makes no impression on the pit; similarly, we remember very little of what we learn.

13. See the parallel text in Genesis Rabbah 45.7.

14. A parallel text in BT Sanhedrin (106b) has the following in the place of the last two sentences: "But it is because the Holy One, blessed be He, requires the heart, as it is written, *But the Lord looketh on the heart*" (1 Sam. 16:7).

15. R. Nahman uses the same expression in a similar context at Hullin 93b.

16. Mishnah Sotah 9:15 might also be mentioned in connection with the idea of the decline of the generations. There the death of various teachers is connected with the disappearance from humanity of the qualities which they embodied.

17. As Jose Faur aptly comments concerning the Talmudic rabbis: "The whole notion of a system, let alone systematic attention, was alien to them." See Faur's "Monoligualism and Judaism," *Cardozo Law Review* 14 (1993): 1712–44, p. 1724.

18. See Shmuel Safrai (ed.), *The Literature of the Sages* (Philadelphia: Fortress Press, 1987), pp. 303–04 for sources.

19. This text, it should be noted, was quoted by R. Yomtov Lippman Heller (1574–1654), *Tosfot Yomtov* to Eduyot I.5, as refuting the claim that previous generations were necessarily superior to later ones.

20. It should be noted that in every place in the BT where this mishnah is quoted, it is assumed that no court can in fact be greater in *both* wisdom and number than earlier courts. See Megillah 2a, Gittin 36b, and Avodah Zarah 36a. The selfsame situation obtains with respect to JT. See Avodah Zarah II.8 and Sabbath I.4 Although it may very well be that these texts assume that no later court can be greater than any previous court in wisdom, that is not what they say; they may very well have held that no later courts were as great in number as earlier courts. Thus, these passages in the Talmud cannot be taken as necessarily affirming the decline of the generations. The commentaries generally raise the question, since all Great Sanhedrin

have the same number of members, how can one be greater in number than another? Two of the most prevalent answers are that the expression refers to the number of scholars flourishing in the generation of the court, or to the number of students of the members of the court.

21.   The passage continues, comparing Moses and Ezra through the use of further verses. For parallels, see JT Megillah 1:9 and Tosefta Sanhedrin IV.

22.   Rashi reads the passage in a way which may be thought to negate this possibility. How could R. Akiva teach "laws given to Moses at Sinai" which Moses did not know? The answer given by Rashi is that these were laws which Moses had not yet received at the point in his life when this episode took place. This might solve the logical problem posed by the text, but in no way removes its sting, since Akiva still expounded heaps and heaps of laws (apparently unknown to Moses) on each tittle of each letter in the Torah; Moses was also unable to follow R. Akiva's discussion and only at a relatively late point in that discussion did R. Akiva get to a law given to Moses at Sinai. Thus, my conclusion stands: Moses is here presented as acknowledging R. Akiva's superiority.

23.   Parallels: JT Avodah Zarah 5:1, Gen. Rabbah 24, Exod. Rabbah 40:2, and Lev. Rabbah 26.

24.   Joseph withstood the attempt by Potiphar's wife to seduce him.

25.   Boaz refused to take advantage of Ruth.

26.   See II Sam. 3:15–16. Palti lived for a long time with Saul's daughter Michal without having sexual relations with her.

27.   Who "eschewed the pleasures of women in their eagerness to study Torah" (Soncino).

28.   On this Rashi comments that the generations of Moses and Joshua "greatly concerned themselves with Torah, the generation of Hezekiah, more than they . . . "

29.   There are various other passages which can be construed in this fashion, although they are rather less clear than those I have cited here. See, for example, BT Kiddushin 72b, where it is stated that "a righteous man [*zaddik*] does not leave the world [i.e., die] until another righteous man like him [*ke-moto*] has been created." The use of the verse, *the sun rises and the sun sets* (Eccles. 1:5) in this connection strengthens the idea that *ke-moto* in this passage really means "like him" and not just "in place of him" (since it is the same sun which both rises and sets). The text speaks explicitly among others of the passing of Rabbi Judah the Prince, a tanna, and the birth of Rav Judah, an amora. Thus, Rav Judah "was like" Rabbi Judah the Prince, replacing him in the world. Such a statement could not, it seems, have been made by someone who held strictly to the idea of the decline of the generations, whether in a single period, or between periods (as was the case with this example). The well-known text from Hullin 6b–7a, "It must therefore be that his ancestors left something undone whereby he [King Hezekiah] might distinguish himself; so in my case, my ancestors left room for me to distinguish myself," is not, I think, strictly relevant to our

issue, since it really says nothing about the relative status of ancestors vis à vis descendents.

30. See Ya'akov Blidstein, "The Concept of Oral Law in R. Scherira's Epistle," *Da'at* 4 (1980): 5–16 (Hebrew). On p. 6 Blidstein argues that the *Iggeret* stakes out a clear-cut religious/ideological position and on p. 10 writes that according to Rav Sherira, the entire corpus of Talmudic literature is a consequence of the decline of the generations; as the generations become less and less talented, the need to create a detailed literature grew.

31. Rav Sherira's *Iggeret* has had a complicated history. See B. M. Lewin (ed.), *Iggeret Rav Sherira Gaon* (Haifa, 1921), pp. i–lxxi. I cite here the Engish translation of Nossin Dovid Rabinowich, *The Iggeres of Rav Sherira Gaon* (Jerusalem: Moznaim, 1988); as with the other translations I quote in this study, I have allowed myself the liberty of emending the translation without calling attention to that in each place. See also Nossin Dovid Rabinowich, trans., *The Iggeres of Rav Sherira Gaon* (Jerusalem: Vagshal, 1991) (Hebrew translation). Citations from the *Iggeret* will list the page in Lewin's text and in Rabinowich's two translations.

32. Lewin, p. 13; Rabinowich, English, p. 8, Hebrew, p. 22. This should be contrasted with Rav Sherira's observation (Lewin, p. 10; Rabinowich, English, p. 5, Hebrew, p. 20) that before the destruction of the second temple, "wisdom was abundant."

33. Lewin, p. 20; Rabinowich, English, p. 16, Hebrew p. 31. For a parallel text, see *Seder Olam* in Adolph Neubauer ed., *Mediaeval Jewish Chronicles*, vol. 1 (Oxford: Clarendon Press, 1887), p. 173.

34. See Lewin, p. 29, Rabinowich, Hebrew, p. 41, English, p. 27 where both R. Akiva and R. Meir were said to have "broad hearts" (*rahav lev*). This passage may also refer to the text from Eruvin 53a, cited above, to the effect that "the hearts of the earlier scholars were like the door of the *Ulam* . . . "

35. Lewin, p. 52; Rabinowich, English, p. 58, Hebrew, p. 70; compare also Lewin, p. 53; Rabinowich, English, p. 60, Hebrew, p. 71: "The later sages also needed other things that the earlier sages had not needed . . . "

36. Lewin, p. 62; Rabinowich, English, p. 73, Hebrew, p. 84.

37. Michael S. Berger, "The Authority of the Babylonian Talmud . . . ," p. 30 makes the same point, and offers interesting suggestions concerning R. Sherira's strategy in countering the Karaite threat.

38. For an illuminating discussion of aspects of this point, see Gerald J. Blidstein, "Oral Law as Institution in Maimonides," in Ira Robinson, *et al.*, eds., *The Thought of Moses Maimonides* (Lewiston: Edwin Mellen Press) 1990 (= *Studies in the History of Philosophy* 17): 167–82.

39. For a study on Maimonides' attitude towards the Gaonim, see Meir Havazelet, *Maimonides and the Gaonites* (Jerusalem/New York: Sura, 1967) (Hebrew). Havazelet cites expressions found both in Rav Sherira's *Iggeret* and in the writings of

Maimonides (see, for example, p. 212), but in the absence of express references to Rav Sherira in the writings of Maimonides or quotations from his works, it is not possible to determine whether or not Maimonides was familiar with the *Iggeret*.

40. Collecting all the relevant texts and analyzing them would, of course, be an important and interesting project in and of itself, particularly if one paid attention to the differences and similarities between Asheknazi and Sefardi figures and sought connections between the various positions held and contemporary historical and social phenomena.

41. Note that Tosafot, *ha-yamim ha-rishonim* . . . accept the idea of the decline of the generations here as well, commenting that the verse might be used to justify the claim that one should attend to the words of the earlier generations over those of the latter; "do not say this, since you only have the judge who is in your day." See Havlin, "On Literary Sealing . . . " (above, note 4) p. 171, note 99 for discussion of these passages. For literature on the attitude of the Tosafot to our question, see Ephraim Kanarfogel, *Jewish Education and Society in the High Middle Ages* (Detroit: Wayne State University Press, 1992), pp. 171–72.

42. Further on Rashi on this issue, see Yonah Frankel, *Darko shel Rashi be-Ferusho le-Talmud ha-Bavli* (Jerusalem: Magnes, 1980), pp. 29–32. Rashi does not accept the idea of the decline of the generations in any simple sense. As Frankel notes (p. 31, note 51), in a comment to Niddah 7b, *s.v., ha-ka'mashma lan*, Rashi maintains that the Amoraim were more careful [*dikdaku*] in determining the specific halakhot than were the Tannaim. For use of the idea of decline by Abraham ibn Ezra (1089–1164), a generation after Rashi, see the text cited by Shraga Abramson on pp. 30–31 in "On the History of the Medieval Literary Debate on *Hagavei ha-Sela*," *Sinai* 87 (1980): 25–33 (Hebrew); my thanks to Prof. Ya'akov Blidstein for this reference.

43. See Rabbenu Nissim ben Reuben Gerondi, *Derashot*, edited by Leon A. Feldman (Jerusalem: Shalem, 1973), eighth derashah, pp. 126–27.

44. Further on Alashkar and this responsum, see Louis Jacobs, *Theology in the Responsa* (London: Routledge and Kegan Paul, 1975), p. 131. For a survey of the consequences of the acceptance of the doctrine of decline of the generations on medieval responsa literature, see Zimmels (above, note 1). For a facinating and remarkable responsum relevant to our issue see *Teshuvot ha-Radbaz* IV.94 (= #1165). In this responsum Rabbi David ben Solomon ibn Abi Zimra (1479–1573) maintains that his generation of Egyptian Jews is superior to the generation of Maimonides (1138–1204). He recognizes the problematic character of this claim, given the doctrine of the decline of the generations, and seeks to find an historical explanation for this suprising improvement. Explanations aside, in the end he insists that he cannot deny the evidence of his own eyes. My thanks to Shmuel Morrell for drawing my attention to this source.

45. On Karo's view of the decline of the generations, see Isadore Twersky, "The Shulhan 'Aruk: Enduring Code of Jewish Law," *Judaism* 16 (1967): 141–58, p. 142.

46. There are significant textual variants here, but they do not concern us.

47. I cite the translation (emended) of Moses Hyamson, *Mishneh Torah, The Book of Adoration by Maimonides* (Jerusalem: Boys Town Jerusalem Publishers, 1962).

48. It is interesting to note that Karo introduces his conception in his commentary to the *Arba'ah Turim*, the *Bet Yosef*, but not in his commentary to the *Mishneh Torah*, the *Kesef Mishnah*. This is actually not surprising; the *Kesef Mishnah* is a commentary on Maimonides and in it R. Karo largely does that: comment on Maimonides. The *Bet Yosef*, as its author explains in his Introduction to it, is actually an independent work, following the organizational framework of the *Arba'ah Turim*. It should be further noted that in his gloss on Maimonides' "Laws of the Rebellious Elder," II.1 Karo seems to be aware that Maimonides does not accept the decline of the generations. Karo's comment will be dicussed below.

49. See also Benjamin Blech, "Learning from Heretics," *Tradition* 25 (1990): 12–17, p. 14 for an example of the attribution of the idea of the decline of the generations to R. Karo by his commentator R. Shabbtai Cohen (Shakh).

50. See Gerald (Ya'akov) Blidstein, *Ha-Tefillah be-Mishnato ha-Hilkhatit shel ha-Rambam* (Jerusalem: Mossad Bialik, 1994), p. 114. For background specific to the debate on the recitation of the *sh'ma*, see pp. 101–03.

51. The Maharal's *Be'er ha-Golah* was published by Pardes in Tel Aviv in 1967. It is not that ideas similar to those of the Maharal's were unknown in the Middle Ages, but his is the most throughly worked out exposition of the doctrine. For a similar but much briefer medieval treatment, see the text cited by Dov Schwartz from *Zedah la-Derekh* by R. Menahem ben Zerah, one of the students of the Rashba, on p. 151 of "Rationalism and Conservatism: The Philosophy of R. Solomon ben Adreth's Circle," *Da'at* 32–33 (1994): 143–82 (Hebrew).

52. It is a very safe bet that the Maharal meant Jews, not humans generally.

53. For background on Maharal's *Be'er ha-Golah* see Mordecai Breuer, "Maharal of Prague's Dispute with the Christians—A New Look at *Sefer Be'er ha-Golah*," *Tarbiz* 55 (1985): 253–60 (Hebrew), and the sources cited there. Breuer shows that part of Maharal's intention in writing the book was to defend the Talmud against attacks of Christians and apostate Jews.

54. Moses Hayyim Luzzatto, *Mesilat Yesharim: The Path of the Upright*, ed., and trans. Mordecai M. Kaplan (Philadelphia: Jewish Publication Society, 1936), chapter 22, pp. 197–98.

55. David Nieto, *Ha-Kuzari ha-Sheni, Matteh Dan*, edited by Y. L. Maimon (Jerusalem: Mossad ha-Rav Kook, 1958), p. 68. For a recent study of Nieto, and references to the scholarly literature upon him, see David Ruderman, "Jewish Thought in Newtonian England: The Career and Writings of David Nieto," *PAAJR* 58 (1992): 193–219.

56. In offering this explanation, of course, Nieto *assumes* that attributing the doctrine of the decline of the generations to Abbaye is not problematic, while at-

tributing to him another doctrine would be problematic. Dwarves are smaller than giants, but sometimes they can see farther.

57.   See Avraham Melamed, "The Sources of the Image of the Locust and the Giant in R. Abraham ibn Ezra's 'Nedod ha-Sir Oni," *Jerusalem Studies in Hebrew Literature* 13 (1992): 95–102 (Hebrew).

58.   Robert K. Merton has traced the history of the expression through European literature in an amusing book, *On the Shoulders of Giants: A Shandean Postscript* (New York: Harcourt, Brace, and World, 1965). Uses of the expression in the context of halakhah were studied by Israel Ta-Shema in " '*Hilkhita ki-Batrai*'— Historical Aspects of a Legal Maxim," *Annual of Hebrew Law* 6–7 (1979/80): 405–23 (Hebrew); and in the context of the sociology of knowledge by Hillel Levine, "Dwarfs on the Shoulders of Giants—A Case Study in the Impact of Modernization on the Social Epistemology of Judaism," *JSS* 40 (1978): 63–72. A number of scholars have made a hobby of tracing the expression in Hebrew literature. See the articles by Dov Zlotnick, "The Commentary of Rabbi Abraham Azulai to the Mishnah," *PAAJR* 40 (1972): 147–68; and "On the Source of the Parable, 'The Dwarf and the Giant' and its Development," *Sinai* 77 (1975): 186–89 (Hebrew); and the comments by Tuvia Freschel in *Ha-Doar*, 11 Iyyar 5734, p. 425 and 29 Tevet 5736, p. 136 and in *Sinai* 78 (1976), p. 288. See also Y. Elbaum, "On the Source of the Allegory of the Dwarf and the Giant and its Development," *Sinai* 77 (1975): 132 (Hebrew). See most recently, S. Z. Leiman, "Dwarfs on the Shoulders of Giants," *Tradition* 27 (1993): 90–94.

59.   P. 69. I assume this to mean that Nieto understands the Kabbalists to hold that the tribulations are a consequence of diminishing intellect.

60.   Viewing Nieto against the intellectual currents of the Jewish world of his time would flesh out our understanding of his position on this issue, but it is not stricly necessary for our purposes here. According to a penetrating and facinating study by Shalom Rosenberg, Nieto wrote his work in response to what Rosenberg calls a "Protestant" movement among seventeenth-century Jewish intellectuals. See Rosenberg, "Emunat Hakhamim," Isadore Twersky and Bernard Septimus eds., *Jewish Thought in the Seventeenth Century* (Cambridge: Harvard University Press, 1987): 285–341, esp. pp. 289, 294, and 310–11.

61.   As I will note below in chapter 7, there is good reason to suspect that present day emphasis on the decline of the generations in traditionalist circles reflects a similar situation.

Chapter 2: Maimonides on Nature and Miracles

1.   Emphasis added.

2.   Emphasis added. Compare also II.30, p. 353, where Maimonides explains that the work of creation was called *good* because it subsists "in durable, perpetual,

and permanent fashion." The world is everlasting, it should be noted, because God so wills it. In principle, as I understand the matter, Maimonides' God *could* bring the universe to an end.

3. On *Nomoi*, see my "Revelation and Messianism: A Maimonidean Study," in Dan Cohn-Sherbok (ed.), *Torah and Revelation* (New York: Edwin Mellen Press, 1992): 117–33.

4. My thanks to Roy Pinchot for suggesting this line of thought to me. This is a good place to emphasize that Maimonides explicitly accepts a position which he attributes to Aristotle (as formulated by Alexander), according to which God's providence over species is expressed through their stability and permanence. Thus, individuals (of course) are not stable or permanent, and individual human beings can change; species, however, do not. Thus, the human species cannot itself be in a state of constant decline. See *Guide of the Perplexed* III.17, pp. 465 and 471–72.

5. This is not really entirely relevant, but it is more than likely that Maimonides would have a hard time accepting contemporary rabbinic doctrine that eggs, olives, etc. were larger in the time of Talmud than they are today. For quite a remarkable expression of this, see Rabbi Yehezkel Landau (the "Noda be-Yehudah") in his *Ziyyun le-Nefesh Hayyah al Massekhet Pesahim* (Jerusalem, 1976), p. 236, where he argues that eggs must have gotten smaller, since fingers could not have gotten bigger (at issue was the relation between the sizes of fingers and eggs), since "the generations are diminishing." My thanks to Elhanan Adler for this reference.

6. This may be the place to note that supporters of the doctrine of the decline of the generations tend to ignore the non-Jewish world altogether, paying no attention to the question of whether or not non-Jews have also suffered the same sort of decline and degeneration they attribute to Jews. This point alone should make it clear that the notion of the decline of the generations would not be easily accepted by most medieval Jewish philosophers, whose approach to the world was, as Alfred Ivry insightfully pointed out, "shockingly neutral" from the perspective of most of their co-religionists. See Ivry, "Philosophical Translations from the Arabic in Hebrew During the Middle Ages," in *Recontres de cultures dans la philosophie médiévale: traductions et traducteurs de l'antiquité tardive au xiv siècle* (Louvain-La-Neuve: Universite Catholique de Louvain, 1990): 167–86, p. 184.

7. One might also argue that decline is not a miracle, but part of nature. Instead of "ontogeny recapitulating phylogeny" why couldn't phylogeny recapitulate ontogeny? After all, individual humans grow ever more decrepit with age; why could not the human race? This hardly meshes with Maimonides' understanding of the settled natures of created beings as discussed in the previous section; it also runs counter to his view of history as involving what we would call today "human progress," as I will discuss below in chapter five.

8. This claim is supported in detail in my *Maimonides on Judaism and the Jewish People* (Albany: SUNY Press, 1991).

9. Helpful studies on the subject include Joseph Heller, "Maimonides' Theory of Miracle," Alexander Altmann (ed.), *Between East and West* (London: East and West

Library, 1958): 112–27; Basil Herring, *Joseph ibn Kaspi's Gevia Kesef: A Study in Medieval Jewish Philosophic Bible Commentary* (New York: Ktav, 1982), pp. 101–06; Howard Kreisel, "Miracles in Medieval Jewish Philosophy," *JQR* 75 (1984): 99–133; Aviezer Ravitzky, "The Anthropological Theory of Miracles in Medieval Jewish Philosophy," Isadore Twersky ed., *Studies in Medieval Jewish History and Literature*, vol. 2 (Cambridge: Harvard University Press, 1984): 231–72; Michael Zvi Nehorai, "Maimonides on Miracles," *Shlomo Pines Jubilee Volume on the Occasion of his Eightieth Birthday, Part II* (=*Jerusalem Studies in Jewish Thought* 9) (Jerusalem: Hebrew University, 1990): 1–18 (Hebrew); and Eliezer Schweid, *Ta'am ve-Hakashah* (Ramat Gan: Massada, 1970): 172–206 (Hebrew).

10.   I cite the text as translated in *Ethical Writings of Maimonides*, edited by Raymond L. Weiss and Charles Butterworth (New York: New York University Press, 1975), p. 87.

11.   The references here are to the text of the Mishnah.

12.   I cite from *The Commentary to Mishnah Aboth* trans. Arthur David (New York: Bloch, 1968), pp. 100–01, with considerable emendations.

13.   See Kreisel, "Miracles in Medieval Jewish Philosophy," p. 109n for a discussion of the term (*gharib*) translated here as "strange;" the use of the term does not mean that Maimonides rejected the doctrine being put forward.

14.   I cite from the translation of Abraham Halkin in *Crisis and Leadership: Epistles of Maimonides* (Philadelphia: Jewish Publication Society, 1985), p. 223.

15.   Pp. 231–32.

16.   P. 232.

17.   As we shall see below, Maimonides believed that various kinds of decline and degeneration had indeed taken place among the Jews; but in every place where he posits such decline he indeed offers sociological or historical, not metaphysical, explanations.

18.   My argument here is not with Maimonides, of course, who knew not computers, but with his contemporary interpreters who use them.

Chapter 3: Maimonides on Decline

1.   Fred Rosner trans., *Moses Maimonides' Commentary on the Mishnah— Introduction to Seder Zeraim and Commentary on Tractate Berachoth* (New York: Feldheim, 1975), pp. 117–18. The text is found in Rabbi J. Kafih's *Mishnah im Perush Rabbenu Moshe ben Maimon* (Jerusalem: Mossad ha-Rav Kook, 1963), pp. 20–21. Further on Maimonides' attitude towards aggadah, see his comments in his commentary to Mishnah Sanhedrin X.1 (*Perek Helek*). See Rav Kafih's edition, pp. 200–202, and for an English translation, Isadore Twersky, *A Maimonides Reader* (New York: Behrman House, 1972), pp. 407–10.

2. Introduction to Tohorot, Kafih, pp. 33–34, 37; I cite the translation of Isadore Twersky, *Introduction to the Mishneh Torah of Maimonides* (New Haven: Yale University Press, 1980), p. 278.

3. I cite the text as translated in Isadore Twersky, *A Maimonides Reader* (New York: Behrman House, 1972), pp. 407–09. The original Arabic may be found in Rabbi Kafih's dual language edition on pp. 200–02. On the question of medieval attitudes towards *Aggadah* generally see the following studies: Marc Saperstein, *Decoding the Rabbis* (Cambridge: Harvard University Press, 1980), pp. 1–20; Bernard Saperstein, " 'Open Rebuke and Concealed Love': Nahmanides and the Andalusian Tradition," in Isadore Twersky ed., *Rabbi Moses Nahmanides (Ramban): Explorations in His Religious and Literary Virtuosity* (Cambridge: Harvard University Press, 1983): 11–34; Marvin Fox, "Nahmanides on the Status of Aggadot: Perspectives on the Disputation at Barcelona, 1263," *Journal of Jewish Studies* 40 (1989): 95–109; and Elliot R. Wolfson, "By Way of Truth: Aspects of Nahmanides' Kabbalistic Hermeneutic," *AJSReview* 14 (1989): 103–78, pp. 153–78.

4. *Book of Commandments*, translated by Charles B. Chavel, vol. 2 (London: Soncino, 1967), p. 365.

5. "Letter on Astrology," translated by Ralph Lerner in Lerner and Muhsin Mahdi eds., *Medieval Political Philosophy* (Ithaca: Cornell University Press, 1972), p. 229. On this text, see Jacob I. Dienstag, "Maimonides' Letter on Astrology to the Rabbis of Southern France," *Kiryat Sefer* 61 (1987): 147–58 (Hebrew).

6. I cite the translation of Moses Hyamson, *Book of Knowledge* (New York: Feldheim, 1974), p. 4b.

7. Compare further "Laws of Moral Qualities," VI.1 in which Maimonides mentions in passing that in his day all the nations of which he knew or had heard reports behaved improperly.

8. I cite the translation of A. M. Hershman, *The Book of Judges* (New Haven: Yale University Press, 1949), p. 72.

9. See "Epistle to Yemen," near the beginning. I cite the translation of A. S. Halkin in Halkin and David Hartman, *Crisis and Leadership* (Philadelphia: Jewish Publication Society, 1985), p. 95. See further, p. 117: "Remember that this low state of learning and science is not peculiar to your country, but is widely prevalent in Israel today."

10. See Leon D. Stitskin, ed. and trans. *Letters of Maimonides* (New York: Yeshiva University Press, 1977), "Letter to the Sages of Lunel," pp. 163–66, pp. 164–65. For the original Hebrew source, see Y. Shailat ed., *Iggerot ha-Rambam* vol. 2 (Jerusalem: Ma'aliyot, 1988), p. 558–59. For other pessimistic views of the times in which Maimonides lived, see the sources cited by Bernard Septimus in *Hispano-Jewish Culture in Transition: The Career and Controversies of Ramah* (Cambridge: Harvard University Press, 1982), p. 26; see also, p. 39.

11. Here is not the place to go into the question of what Maimonides means by "wisdom" [*hokhmah*] and its relation to Talmud. By emphasizing the word "and" i⸱

this sentence I have hinted at my understanding of Maimonides' words here. Further on this subject, see Hannah Kasher, "Talmud Torah as a Means of Apprehending God in Maimonides' Teachings," *Jerusalem Studies in Jewish Thought* 5 (1986): 71–81 (Hebrew) and my *Maimonides on Human Perfection* (Atlanta: Scholars Press, 1990), pp. 7–39.

12.   On this criticism, see the articles by Havlin cited above in chapter 1, note 4 and Havazelet's *Maimonides and the Gaonites*, cited above in chapter 1, note 39.

13.   For the necessary qualifications on this statement, see my "The Conception of the Torah as a Deductive Science in Medieval Jewish Thought," *Revue des etudes juives* 146 (1987): 265–79; and "Gersonides on the Song of Songs and the Nature of Science," *Journal of Jewish Thought and Philosophy* 4 (1994): 1–21.

14.   As the Gemara ad loc. notes, the text is ambiguous and could mean in front of three students or in the presence of three people (the teacher included) altogether.

15.   See Rabbi Kafih's text. As he notes there, this passage is missing from the standard translations, probably because of homeoleuteton.

16.   I, Introduction, p. 6.

17.   Arabic: *al-ilm al-ilahi*; the commonly accepted term in medieval Arabic for 'metaphysics' and the same term used by Maimonides in his commentary on Hagigah. Maimonides, in his *Art of Logic*, XIV explicitly defines "divine science" as "metaphysics" (*ma ba'da al-tabia*). For the Arabic text of *Art of Logic* (*Millot ha-Higayon*) see Israel Efros, "Maimonides' Arabic Treatise on Logic," *PAAJR* 34 (1966): 9–42 (Hebrew section) and 155–60 (English section); the text in question here appears on p. 40. In general, see Harry A. Wolfson, "The Classification of Sciences in Mediaeval Jewish Philosophy," in his *Studies in the History and Philosophy of Religion* I (Cambridge: Harvard University Press, 1973): 493–545.

18.   Hagigah 14b. For further detail on Maimonides' identification of *ma'aseh bereshit* with physics and *ma'aseh merkavah* with metaphysics, see my *Maimonides on Judaism and the Jewish People* (Albany: SUNY Press, 1991), pp. 65–72.

19.   He was, of course, criticized for doing precisely that. See, for example, the following statement by Rabbi Samson Raphael Hirsch:

[Maimonides] sought to reconcile Judaism with the difficulties which confronted it from without, instead of developing it creatively from within, for all the good and the evil which bless and afflict the heritage of the father. His peculiar mental tendency was Arabic-Greek, and his conception of the purpose of life the same. He entered into Judaism from without, bringing with him opinions of whose truth the had convinced himself from extraneous sources and—he reconciled. For him, too, self-perfecting through the knowledge of truth was the highest aim, the practical he deemed subordinate. For him knowledge of God was the end, not the means; hence he devoted his intellectual powers to speculations upon the Deity, and sought to bind Judaism to the results of his speculative investigations as to postulates of science or faith. The Mizvoth became for him merely ladders, necessary only to conduct to knowledge or to protect against error.

See R. Samson Raphael Hirsch, *The Nineteen Letters of Ben Uziel*, translated by Bernard Drachman (New York: Funk and Wagnalls, 1899), eighteenth letter, pp. 181–82.

20.   Leo Strauss, "Progress or Return: The Contemporary Crisis in Western Civilization," *Modern Judaism* 1 (1981): 17–34, p. 23.

21.   Isadore Twersky, "Some Non-Halakic Aspects of the *Mishneh Torah*," Alexander Altmann ed., *Jewish Medieval and Renaissance Studies* (Cambridge: Harvard University Press, 1967): 95–118, pp. 114–15. For background on this issue, see N. Roth, "The 'Theft of Philosophy' by the Greeks from the Jews," *Classical Folia* 32 (1978): 53–67.

22.   Shlomo Pines, "Translator's Introduction," in his translation of the *Guide of the Perplexed*, p. cxxxiii.

23.   This approach is adopted by Lawrence V. Berman in a review of the Pines translation of the *Guide of the Perplexed*, *Journal of the American Oriental Society* 85 (1965): 410–13, p. 413.

24.   Harry A. Wolfson, *Philo*, vol. 1 (Cambridge: Harvard University Press, 1962), p. 163.

25.   Fred Rosner trans., *Moses Maimonides' Commentary on the Mishnah— Introduction to the Mishnah and Tractate Berachoth* (New York: Feldheim, 1975), pp. 111–14; corresponds to R. Joseph Kafih ed. and trans., *Mishnah im Perush Rabbenu Mosheh ben Maimon*, vol. 1 (Jerusalem: Mossad ha-Rav Kook, 1963), p. 19.

26.   See Maimonides' commentary on *Helek* for his attitude towards those who so denigrate aggadah. In Twersky's *A Maimonides Reader* the text is on p. 408.

27.   *Guide of the Perplexed* II.11, p. 276.

28.   I assume that Maimonides is referring to aggadot here, and perhaps Biblical verses.

29.   On the background of this passage, see Shlomo Pines, "The Limitations of Human Knowledge According to Al-Farabi, ibn Bajjah, and Maimonides," in Isadore Twersky (ed.), *Studies in Medieval Jewish History and Literature*, vol. 1 (Cambridge: Harvard University Press, 1979): 82–109, pp. 100–104.

30.   On the basis of the closing passages in I.70 I take Maimonides to mean: God's existence and relation to the created world.

31.   On Maimonides' theory of providence, see my *Maimonides on Judaism and the Jewish People*, pp. 23–26 and the sources cited there.

32.   For Maimonides' attitude on astrology, see Gad Freudenthal, "Maimonides' Astrology in Context: Cosmology, Physics, Medicine, and Providence," in Fred Rosner

and Samuel Kottek eds., *Moses Maimonides: Physician, Scientist, and Philosopher* (Northvale, NJ: Jason Aronson, 1993): 77–90.

33.   See below, in the next section.

34.   The Hebrew original is in Shailat, *Iggerot ha-Rambam* Vol. 2, p. 480. For an English paraphrase, see Stitskin, *Letters of Maimonides*, pp. 119–20.

35.   The prayer book, it should be remembered, not only *expresses* the opinions of the Rabbis who created it, but also powerfully *shapes* the views of subsequent generations. The view expressed here may not be the only rabbinic explanation for the catastrophe of destruction and exile, but its place in the liturgy made it the most widely known and accepted.

36.   This is a precise analogue of Maimonides' understanding of the nature of reward and punishment for individuals.

37.   Maimonides quotes this expression in many of his writings. It is derived from Avodah Zarah 54b:

> Our Rabbis taught: philosophers asked the elders in Rome, "If your God has no desire for idolatry, why does He not abolish it?" They replied, "If it was something of which the world has no need that was worshipped, He would abolish it; but people worship the sun, moon, stars, and planets; should He destroy the universe on account of fools!" The world follows its natural course.

Maimonides uses it the eighth of his "Eight Chapters"; in *Guide of the Perplexed* II.29, p. 345; in "Laws of Kings," XII.1, and near the end of his "Treatise on Resurrection" (Halkin trans. in *Crisis and Leadership*, p. 223).

38.   I quote from the translation of Moses Hyamson, *The Book of Adoration* (Jerusalem: Boys Town Publishers, 1962).

39.   For detailed analysis of these texts and their background, see Blidstein, *Ha-Tefilah*, pp. 38–47.

40.   Twersky, "Some Non-Halakic Apects of the *Mishneh Torah*," p. 112.

41.   I say "failure" here and not "refusal" in order to emphasize that as I understand him, Maimonides was not consciously rejecting a position he felt to be otherwise widely held in Judaism. It was the point of the first chapter of this book to suggest that such was not the case.

Chapter 4: Maimonides' Attitude towards the Authority of the Rabbis in non-Halakhic Matters

1.   Pines cites Pesahim 94b.

2.   Pines cites *On the Heavens* ii.9.290b.12ff.

3. Pines cites Pesahim 94b. Maimonides' use of this passage here should be contrasted with that of R. Isaac Abravanel (1437–1508), for example, who tries to show that the Rabbis were *not* mistaken on this issue. The text may be found in his Commentary to Genesis 1, p. 57 of the Jerusalem, 1964 edition of his commentary.

4. *Guide of the Perplexed*, II.8, p. 267.

5. And, as Maimonides says, "For only truth pleases Him, may He be exalted, and only that which is false angers him" (*Guide of the Perplexed* II.48, p. 409). In his commentary on *Helek* Maimonides comments that "one should believe the truth for the sake of the truth." One who does that "serves God out of love." The passage is in Rav Kafih's dual language edition on p. 199 and in Isadore Twersky, *A Maimonides Reader*, p. 406.

6. *Pirkei Mosheh*, chapter 25. I quote from the translation of George Sarton in "Maimonides: Philosopher and Physician," *Bulletin of the Cleveland Medical Library* 2 (1955): 3–22; reprinted in Dorothy Stimson (ed.), *Sarton on the History of Science* (Cambridge: Harvard University Press, 1962): 78–101. The passage quoted appears on p. 89 of the reprint. In Fred Rosner's translation (*The Medical Aphorisms of Maimonides*, Vol. 2, translated and edited by Fred Rosner and Suessman Muntner [New York: Yeshiva University, 1971]) the passage appears on pp. 218–19. The Arabic original of Maimonides' *Medical Aphorisms*, known in Hebrew as *Pirkei Mosheh*, has never been published in its entirety. Portions of the Arabic text of the twenty-fifth chapter, with modern Hebrew translation, appear in Y. Kafih, ed. and trans., *Iggerot ha-Rambam* (Jerusalem: Mossad ha-Rav Kook, 1972), pp. 148–67. Two medieval Hebrew translations were edited by Suessmann Muntner in Moshe ben Maimon (Maimonides) *Medical Works*, Vol. 2: *Medical Aphorisms of Moses* (Jerusalem: Mossad ha-Rav Kook, 1959).

7. "Letter on Astrology," p. 229.

8. I.e., Maimonides had just proven that rejection of astrology is "one of the roots of the religion of Moses our Master" (p. 234).

9. "Letter on Astrology," p. 235.

10. The text is found in *Ma'amar al Odot Derashot Hazal* (s.v., *da ki attah hayyav*) printed in many editions of the *Ein Ya'akov*, at the beginning and in *Kovez Tehuvot ha-Rambam ve-Iggerotav* (Leipzig, 1859; photo-edition, Jerusalem, 1967), p. 41a. I quote it as translated by Yehudah Levi, "The Sciences as the 'Maidservants of the Torah' in Maimonides' Writings," Fred Rosner and Samuel Kottek (eds.), *Moses Maimonides: Physician, Scientist, Philosopher* (Northvale: Jason Aronson, 1993): 97–104, p. 103.

11. In this I follow Rabbi Kafih in his notes to his translation of the *Guide of the Perplexed, ad loc.* (Jerusalem: Mossad ha-Rav Kook, 1972).

12. Further on this, see H. J. Zimmels, *Magicians, Theologians, and Doctors* pp. 137–9 and Louis Jacobs, *Theology in the Responsa*, p. 77.

13. *Decoding the Rabbis* (Cambridge: Harvard University Press, 1980), p. 18.

14. This impression is strengthened by the fact that in "Laws of the Foundations of the Torah," IV.13 Maimonides intimates that at least *some* of the readers of the *Mishneh Torah* (not to mention Maimonides himself) could safely navigate *pardes*. On the Hagigah text see the discussion in Gershom Scholem, *Jewish Gnosticism, Merkabah Mysticism, and Talmudic Tradition* (New York: Jewish Theological Seminary, 1965), pp. 14–19.

15. See Shaul Regev, "The Vision of the Nobles of Israel in the Jewish Philosophy of the Middle Ages," *Jerusalem Studies in Jewish Thought* 4 (1984/85): 281–302 (Hebrew).

16. The point of Maimonides' discussion in *Guide of the Perplexed* I.4–5.

17. On Maimonides on "speaking through the holy spirit," see Sara Klein-Braslavi, "Solomon's 'Prophecy' in Maimonides' Writings," in M. Idel, *et al.* eds., *Minhah le-Sarah* (Jerusalem: Magnes, 1994): 57–81 (Hebrew).

18. I do not want to go further into this matter here since it depends upon detailed reading of complicated texts and does not really add substantially to what we have already seen. The matter seems to have been first brought to scholarly attention by Charles Touati in his "Le problème de l'innerance prophétique dans la théologie juive du moyen age," *Revue l'Histoire des Religions* 174 (1968): 169–97. For detailed discussion see Shalom Rosenberg, "On Biblical Interpretation in the *Guide of the Perplexed*," *Jerusalem Studies in Jewish Thought* 1 (1981): 85–157 (Hebrew), pp. 92–93, 143–52. For further discussions, see Warren Zev Harvey, "How to Begin to Study the *Guide of the Perplexed* I.1," *Da'at* 21 (1988): 5–23 (Hebrew), pp. 21–23; and Aviezer Ravitzky, "The Secrets of the *Guide of the Perplexed*: Between the Thirteenth and Twentieth Centuries," in I. Twersky ed., *Studies in Maimonides* (Cambridge: Harvard University Press, 1990): 159–207, pp. 188–89. As noted by Rosenberg, Isaac Abravanel (1437–1508), in his commentary on *Guide of the Perplexed* III. 1–7 (printed at the end of many editions of the *Guide*, under the heading, "*Me-ha-Abravanel le-Helek Shlishi me-ha-Moreh*") attributed to Maimonides the view that Ezekiel made scientific errors. Maimonides is read in the same way by Gersonides (1288–1344) in his commentary on Gen., Venice, 1547, p. 24d (in the edition of Ya'akov Levi [Jerusalem: Mossad ha-Rav Kook, 1992], p. 115; and in the edition of B. Braner and E. Freiman [Jerusalem: Ma'aliyot, 1993], p. 222). Compare further Gersonides' commentary to Job 39:30. Further on Gersonides' own views on prophetic errors in scientific matters, see Charles Touati, *La pensée philosophique et theologique de Gersonide* (Paris: Minuit, 1973), pp. 459–44; and Howard Kreisel, "Theories of Prophecy in Medieval Jewish Philosophy," Ph.D. Diss., Brandeis University, 1981, pp. 226–27.

19. "Laws of Kings and their Wars" XII.2. I cite the translation of A. M. Hershman, *Book of Judges* (New Haven: Yale University Press, 1949).

20. As opposed to "inspired guesses" and certainly as opposed to authoritative pronouncements.

21. *Guide of the Perplexed* I.59, p. 140.

22. Compare the following comment of Ramah (R. Meir Halevi Abulafia), cited by Septimus in *Hispano-Jewish Culture in Transition*, p. 77: "The words of this *beraita* are not a tradition but mere opinion . . . [and since] it would seem that the words of the *tanna* stem from his own deduction one has a right to disagree with this *beraita*." Septimus contrasts this approach with that of "the French anti-rationalists [according to whom] it was axiomatic that anyone who disagreed with an aggadah of the talmudic sages was an *epiqoros*." It must be emphasized that the point at issue here is not that Maimonides, as it were, decided the law (*"paskened"*) according to the majority; in such a case both positions "are the words of the living God"—the rejected position is not thereby seen as false. In our case, Maimonides rejects positions held by individual rabbis because he is convinced that they are false.

23. On which subject see Seymour Feldman, "The End of the Universe in Medieval Jewish Philosophy," *AJSReview* 11 (1986): 53–77.

24. Pines cites BT Rosh ha-Shanah 31a and BT Sanhedrin 97a.

25. I quote from the translation of Ralph Lerner, in Lerner and Muhsin Mahdi eds., *Medieval Political Philosophy*, p. 230. For a detailed exposition and examination of Maimonides' views on astrology, see Y. Tzvi Langermann, "Maimonides' Repudiation of Astrology," *Maimonidean Studies* 2 (1991): 123–58. Further on this see H. Kreisel, "Maimonides' Approach to Astrology," *Proceedings of the Eleventh World Congress of Jewish Studies, Division C*, vol. 2 (Jerusalem: World Union of Jewish Studies, 1994), pp. 25–32 (Hebrew).

26. P. 235; the Hebrew text is in Shailat, *Iggerot ha-Rambam*, vol. 2, p. 488.

27. In actual fact, the truth of astrology seemed to have been unquestioned by the Rabbis; the real question was whether or not astrological influences held sway over the people of Israel. For details, see Alexander Altmann's entry on "astrology" in the *Encyclopaedia Judaica*.

28. Maimonides makes his methodology on this issue clear in his "Treatise on Resurrection: "I fall back on interpreting a statement [allegorically] only when its literal sense is impossible, like the corporeality of God; the possible however, remains as stated" (Halkin trans. in *Crisis and Leadership*, p. 228). Maimonides applies this methodology extensively in the opening chapters of the *Guide of the Perplexed*.

29. I think that I may very well be pushing things too hard here, but it is worth remembering that in other contexts Maimonides excludes from the community of Israel and the world to come individuals who commit errors concerning "roots" of the Torah. See my *Dogma in Medieval Jewish Thought* (Oxford: Oxford University Press, 1986), pp. 17–21; and my *Maimonides on Judaism and the Jewish People*, pp. 59–64.

30. Whose piety and spirituality, it should be remembered, were emphasized in the Talmud. See above, chapter 1, section 2. Piety and spirituality, Maimonides might counter, are not necessarily the ingredients of philosophical acumen. As Pines put it ("Translator's Introduction," p. cxix), Maimonides did not value "saintly simplicity" very highly.

31. For a detailed analysis of this parable, see M. Kellner, *Maimonides on Human Perfection* (Atlanta: Scholars Press, 1990), pp. 13–31.

32. As indicated by the continuation of the text cited from p. 619 and by Maimonides' letter to Joseph with which he opens the *Guide of the Perplexed*, (pp. 3–4).

33. This is as good a place as any to take note of another instance of Maimonides' independence vis-à-vis his predecessors. Avot IV.7 reads: "Rabbi Zadok said, 'Do not fashion it [the Torah] into a crown with which to magnify yourself, nor into a spade with which to dig." On this Maimonides writes, "After I decided that I would not discuss this counsel because it is clear, and also because of my awareness that my teachings concerning it would not appeal to most of the great sages of the Torah, and perhaps to all of them, I revoked my decision and I shall discuss it without regard to either previous or current authorities." It is not unlikely that by "previous" authorities Maimonides meant the Tannaim and Amoraim, since he clearly saw himself as part of the current, Geonic, period. On the whole question of rabbinic salaries, see Ephraim Kanarfogel, "Compensation for the Study of Torah in Medieval Rabbinic Thought," Ruth Link-Salinger ed., *Of Scholars, Savants, and their Texts* (New York: Peter Lang, 1989): 135–48, and the sources cited there. I cite the text from Maimonides' commentary on Avot from Moses Maimonides, *The Commentary to Mishnah Aboth*, Arthur David trans. (New York: Bloch, 1968), p. 71. This may also be the best place to note the interesting, suggestive, and to my mind significant fact that Maimonides nowhere cites the well-known midrash on Deut. 17:11. The passage referring to the authority of Priests, Levites, and judges, states: *thou shalt not turn aside from the sentence which they shall declare unto thee, to the right hand, nor to the left.* On this the Midrash says, "even if they tell you that right is left and left is right" (as cited by Rashi on the verse, quoting from the Sifri). For details, see Gerald Blidstein, " 'Even if He Tells You Right is Left': The Validity of Moral Authority in the *Halakha* and its Limitations," in Moshe Beer ed., *Studies in Halakha and Jewish Thought Presented to Emmanuel Rackman* (Ramat Gan: Bar Ilan University Press, 1994): 221–41 (Hebrew), p. 236.

34. It is my understanding of Maimonides that he rejects the distinction here assumed, between philosophy and religion. My point here and throughout is to show exactly that: time after time, Maimonides arrives at unusual, unpopular, and, in the eyes of many of his coreligionists, downright heterodox views because of antecedently held philosophical positions. But, despite the problems holding these views cause him, he plows ahead, convinced that ultimately Torah and science must teach the same thing. He thus writes esoterically, not because he understood his views as heterodox, but because many of his contemporaries (and ours!) would have so understood him.

Chapter 5: Maimonides on the "Advance" of the Generations

1. I do not mean to impute to Maimonides any sort of modern notion of progress. For a discussion of his views on the subject see my "Maimonides on the

Science of the *Mishneh Torah*—Provisional or Permanent," *AJSReview* 18 (1993): 169–94.

2.   Mekhilta, *Shirata* 3. In the edition of Jacob Z. Lauterbach, *Mekilta de-Rabbi Ishamel,* vol. 2 (Philadelphia: Jewish Publication Society, 1933), p. 24.

3.   As is often the case with midrashim, this one can be read differently (and in a fashion more congenial to Maimonides as I seek to present him in this study): the prophets were indeed greater than the Jews who crossed the Red Sea; nonetheless, the miracle there was so great that "a maid servant saw . . . "

4.   For a discussion of this issue, see my "Messianic Postures in Israel Today," *Modern Judaism* 6 (1986): 197–209, reprinted in Marc Saperstein ed., *Essential Papers on Messianic Movements and Personalities in Jewish History* (New York: New York University Press, 1992): 504–18.

5.   This is especially the case since fine studies on the subject are available. See, for example, Aviezer Ravitzky, "'To the Utmost of Human Capacity': Maimonides on the Days of the Messiah," Joel Kraemer ed., *Perspectives on Maimonides* (Oxford: Oxford University Press, 1991): 209–56.

6.   This is not strictly true of the "Epistle to Yemen," which is certainly the most popular of Maimonides' accounts of the advent of the Messiah. See, for example, p. 125 in Halkin's translation (in *Crisis and Leadership*). But note that Maimonides reiterates his messianic naturalism in another "popular" work, his "Treatise on Resurrection." See Halkin's translation, in *Crisis and Leadership*, p. 222.

7.   While this last is true of Maimonides' account in the *Mishneh Torah*, it is not literally true of his account in the "Epistle to Yemen," where Maimonides says of the Messiah (Halkin trans., p. 121), "Then God will bring him forth . . . " But, as Maimonides makes clear in the *Guide of the Perplexed* (I.66, p. 160) the Torah attributes directly to God actions which are really the natural outgrowth of processes of which God is only the ultimate cause. I take issue here with Shlomo Pines' claim, *Bein Mahshevet Yisrael le-Mahshevet he-Amim* (Jerusalem: Mossad Bialik, 1977), p. 294, that "there is no hint in the *Mishneh Torah* to the effect that normal political causes and means can bring about the ingathering of the exiles . . . " If by this Pines means to impute an overtly miraculous doctrine to Maimonides, then I do not see how he can make that claim, given Maimonides' clear insistence that the coming of the Messiah will involve no miracles, that the only way to know if a king of Israel is the Messiah is if he succeeds in doing what the Messiah is supposed to do, and given the fact that Maimonides places his discussion of the Messiah in the *Mishneh Torah* in the context of "normal" (i.e., non-messianic) kings and their wars. This is not the place to reply if by this Pines means to impute to Maimonides an esoteric doctrine according to which there will be no ingathering of the exiles at all.

8.   For an explication of this admittedly terse statement, see my *Maimonides on Human Perfection*.

9.   Maimonides makes this clear in the one passage in the *Guide of the Perplexed* which deals with the Messiah (III.11, p. 440): "These great evils that com

about between the human individuals who inflict them upon one another because of purposes, desires, opinions, and beliefs are all of them likewise consequent upon privation. For all of them derive from ignorance, I mean from a privation of knowledge." In this chapter, by the way, Maimonides explains the peace which will prevail in the messianic world in naturalistic terms, as a consequence of the spread of knowledge: *the wolf shall dwell with the lamb* (Isaiah 11:6) because *the earth shall be full of the knowledge of the Lord* (Isa. 11:6–9).

10.   Isadore Twersky ed., *A Maimonides Reader* (New York: Behrman House, 1972), pp. 414–15. In Rav Kafih's edition, pp. 207–08.

11.   P. 422.

12.   "Laws of Kings," XI.1; I cite the translation of A. M. Hershman, *Book of Judges*, p. 238.

13.   XI.4; presented by Hershman on pp. xxiii–xxiv. See Hershman's comments there and Leah Naomi Goldfeld, "Laws of Kings, their Wars, and the King Messiah," *Sinai* 91 (1983): 67–79 (Hebrew).

14.   "Laws of Kings," XI.4. The text here is not without its problems, none of which, however, impinge upon our discussion. See Ya'akov Blidstein, "On Universal Rule in Maimonides' Eschatological Vision," in *Arakhim bi-Mivhan ha-Milhamah* (Alon Shevut: Yeshivat Har Ezion, n.d.): 155–72, note 54 (Hebrew). I cite the translation of A. M. Hershman, *Book of Judges*, p. 240.

15.   *Guide of the Perplexed* III.32, p. 526.

16.   Different versions of this passage have been preserved, but these differences are not crucial for our purposes. See Simon-Raymond Schwarzfuchs, "Les lois royales de Maimonide," *REJ* 111 (1951–52): 63–86; and my "On Universalism and Particularism in Judaism," *Da'at* (forthcoming).

17.   If Maimonides truly believed that he lived at the brink of the messianic era, as some maintain, then he obviously believed that human beings not only *could* progress towards the messianic era, but were actually so progressing. On Maimonides' attitude on this matter, see the sources cited in my "A Suggestion Concerning Maimonides' 'Thirteen Principles' and the Status of Non-Jews in the Messianic Era," in Meir Ayali ed., *Tura—Oranim Studies in Jewish Thought: Simon Greenberg Jubilee Volume* (Tel Aviv: Ha-Kibbutz ha-Meuhad, 1986): 249–60 (Hebrew), note 35. Maimonides' pessimistic assessment of the times in which he lived would seem to make this interpretation of his thought problematic, a point I did not appreciate when I wrote that article.

18.   It is my understanding that Maimonides would ultimately reject the distinction drawn here between "philosophical" and "religious" matters; I divide my discussion between the two only for the sake of clarity and convenience.

19.   Hebrew (the Arabic original of the letter is lost): *da'ato*. Another possible translation is "his knowledge." On Maimonides' use of this term, see David Baneth, "Maimonides' Philosophical Terminology," *Tarbiz* 6 (1935): 258–84 (Hebrew), p. 260;

and David R. Blumenthal, "Maimonides on Mind and Metaphoric Language," in D. R. Blumenthal ed., *Approaches to Judaism in Medieval Times* II (Chico: Scholars Press, 1985): 123–32.

20. I quote from Shailat's *Iggerot ha-Rambam*, vol. 2, p. 553. On this letter see Alexander Marx, "Texts By and About Maimonides," *JQR* 25 (1934–5): 374–81; Alfred Ivry, "Islamic and Greek Influences on Maimonides' Philosophy," S. Pines and Y. Yovel (eds.), *Maimonides and Philosophy* (Dordrecht: Martinus Nijhoff, 1986): 139–56; and Shlomo Pines, "Translator's Introduction," p. lix, in Pines' translation of the *Guide of the Perplexed*. Further on this letter and especially on its influence, see Steven Harvey, "Did Maimonides' Letter to Samuel ibn Tibbon Determine Which Philosophers Would be Studied by Later Jewish Thinkers?" *Jewish Quarterly Review* 83 (1992): 51–70.

21. Actually, Maimonides carefully distinguished the Rabbis from the prophets and it would be surprising were he to attribute prophetic abilities to the former. For background and details, see Ephraim Urbach, "Halakhah and Prophecy," *Tarbiz* 19 (1947): 1–27, esp. p. 20 (Hebrew); this article was reprinted with additions in Urbach's *Me-Olamam shel Hakhamim* (Jerusalem: Magnes, 1988): 21–49. In contrast to Maimonides, Halevi expressly connected the two in *Kuzari* III.39. See Nahum Arieli, "Halevi's Conception of Halakhah," *Da'at* 1 (1978): 43–53 (Hebrew). I might note, by the way, that R. Isaac Abravanel (1437–1508) also expressly attributed prophetic inspiration to the Rabbis. See his commentary to Deut. 17 (p. 163 in the Jerusalem, 1964 edition of Abravanel's commentary on the Torah). This may be one more of the many places in which Abravanel consciously adopts positions of Halevi's.

22. See also II. 23 (p. 332). Jose Faur plays down the significance of these passages, interpreting them so as to diminish Maimonides' admiration for Aristotle. See his *Iyyunim ba-Mishneh Torah li-ha-Rambam* (Jerusalem: Mossad ha-Rav Kook, 1978), p. 7. I find Faur's interpretation forced, an estimation reinforced by the fact that Shem Tov ibn Falaquera, Maimonides' great thirteenth century-admirer, criticized the Master for his excessive admiration of Aristotle. See Henry Malter, "Shem Tob ben Joseph Palquera II: His 'Treatise of the Dream'," *JQR* 1 (1910–11): 451–501, p. 492.

23. P. 230; I have slightly emended the translation.

24. This is the burden of Maimonides' refutation of Aristotle's thesis concerning the eternity of the world in *Guide of the Perplexed* II.13–31; see especially chapter 17.

25. Compare also II.3, p. 254. Here we have an example of Maimonides' "whig" interpretation of the history of science.

26. See the texts cited above from *Guide of the Perplexed* II.22 and 24.

27. *The Medical Aphorisms of Maimonides*, vol. 2, translated and edited by Fred Rosner and Suessman Muntner (New York: Yeshiva University, 1971), p. 205.

28. Further on this point, see the discussion in my "On the Status of the Astronomy and Physics in Maimonides' *Mishneh Torah* and *Guide of the Perplexed*: A Chapter in the History of Science," *British Journal for the History of Science* 24 (1991): 453–63.

29. Given Maimonides' attitudes on the true nature of Torah (on which, see my *Maimonides on Judaism and the Jewish People*, pp. 65–79), this is tantamount to saying that gentile scientists in Maimonides' day understood Torah better than the rabbis of his era. This is not a likely interpretation of Maimonides!

30. I do not mean to imply that this growth was a matter of unalloyed progress; there are definitely ups and downs, as evidenced by the texts cited above (chapter 3, section 1) concerning the degradation of Maimonides' own times.

31. On worship in Maimonides as philosophical meditation, see *Guide of the Perplexed* III.51; M. Fox, "Prayer in the Thought of Maimonides," in G. Cohen ed., *Ha-Tefilah ha-Yehudit: Hemshekh vi-Hiddush* (Ramat Gan: Bar Ilan University Press, 1978): 142–67 (Hebrew); and my *Maimonides on Human Perfection*, pp. 31–33. Fox's article is now available in English in his *Interpreting Maimonides* (Chicago: University of Chicago Press, 1990), pp. 297–321.

32. This last point was suggested to me by J. J. Ross. See "Maimonides and Progress—Maimonides' Concept of History," Yehezkel Cohen ed., *Hevrah vi-Historiah* (Jerusalem: Israel Ministry of Education and Culture, 1980): 529–42 (Hebrew).

33. On *semikhah* see Sidney B. Hoenig, *The Great Sanhedrin* (Philadelphia: Dropsie College, 1953), pp. 55 and 248 and J. Newman, *Semikhah [Ordination]: A Study of Its Origin, History, and Function in Rabbinic Literature* (Manchester: Manchester University Press, 1950). More briefly, see Isaac Herzog, *Judaism: Law and Ethics* (London: Soncino, 1974), pp. 127–34.

34. BT Sanhedrin 14a.

35. Fred Rosner trans., *Maimonides' Commentary on the Mishnah, Tractate Sanhedrin* (New York: Sepher-Hermon Press, 1981), pp. 4–5. The text and Hebrew translation are found In Rav Kafih's edition, pp. 147–48.

36. In this he is supported by *Tosafot Yom Tov* to Eduyot I.5.

37. See above, chapter one, note 20.

Chapter 6: On the Nature of the Rabbis' Authority

1. For support of my interpretation of Maimonides' Introduction to the *Mishneh Torah*, and other relevant sources, see Isadore Twersky, *Introduction to the Code of Maimonides* (New Haven: Yale University Press, 1980), pp. 129–30.

2. For studies on this crucial passage, see the sources cited on p. 40 of Lawrence Kaplan, *"Daas Torah*: A Modern Conception of Rabbinic Authority," in Moshe Sokol ed., *Rabbinic Authority and Personal Autonomy* (Northvale, NJ: Jason Aronson, 1992): 1–60.

3. There are other passages (such as the Introduction to the Commentary on the Mishnah, p. 46 [Rosner translation, p. 131]) in which Maimonides speaks of the inherent greatness of the Talmud, going so far as to say that the "spirit of the holy Lord" (Dan. 4:5) can be found in it. I do not think that this reflects a position different than the one expressed here. Aside from the possibility that this is a mere rhetorical flourish, aside from Maimonides' need to emphasize the authority of the Talmud in the face of the Karaite threat, and aside from the possibility that the passage in question refers to Rav Ashi (editor of the Talmud) and not to the Talmud itself (so Rosner understands it), what could Maimonides mean by saying that "the spirit of the holy Lord" is found in a book? Only that the book contains great wisdom, something which he surely believed concerning the Talmud. The Talmud's authority derives from its acceptance; its wisdom helped it to become accepted. Had Maimonides succeeded in his aim in having the *Mishneh Torah* become as widely accepted as the Talmud, would its authority be a consequence of the wisdom to be found in it (i.e., that the "spirit of the holy Lord" can be found in it) or a consequence of its acceptance by the Jews? Clearly the latter, as is evidenced by the fact that Maimonides would not want to say that because his project failed, and the *Mishneh Torah* did not become as widely accepted as the Talmud, we have evidence that the work was defective.

4. Isadore Twersky has shown that Maimonides uses the terms "Mishnah," "Gemara," and "Talmud" in a unique sense. The first two, he points out, "are exactly coterminous in scope—complete, unabridged summaries of the Oral Law." The differences between them are "in method and form . . . " See Twersky, "Some Non-Halakic Aspects . . . " p. 107. This approach helps us to understand how Maimonides could say here that the Sanhedrin ceased to exist only "several years [*mi-kamah shanim*] before the compilation of the Talmud"—by "Talmud" here he may simply have meant the Mishnah. The importance of the connection between the end of the Sanhedrin and the close of the Mishnah is further hinted at in the following passage from the *Guide of the Perplexed* (I.71, pp. 175–76):

> You already know that even the legalistic science of the law was not put down in writing in the olden times because of the precept, which is widely known in the nation: *Words that I have communicated to you orally, you are not allowed to put down in writing* [Gittin 60b]. This precept shows extreme wisdom with regard to the Torah. For it was meant to prevent what has ultimately come about in this respect: I mean the multiplicity of opinions, the variety of schools, the confusions occuring in the expression of what is put down in writing, the negligence that accompanies what is written down, the divisions of the people, who are separated into sects, and the production of confusion with regard to actions. All these matters should be within the authority of *the Great Court of Law*, as we have made clear in our juridicial compilations, and as the text of the Torah shows [Deut. 17:8–12].

Further on Maimonides' ideas on this subject, see Isadore Twersky, "Did R. Abraham ibn Ezra Influence Maimonides?" in Isadore Twersky and Jay M. Harris eds., *Rabbi Abraham ibn Ezra: Studies in the Writings of a Twelfth-Century Jewish Polymath* (Cambridge: Harvard University Press, 1993): 21–48 (Hebrew), p. 36, note 11.

5.   It would take us to far afield to go into the hotly debated question of why Maimonides wrote the *Mishneh Torah*. Let it just be stated that if those scholars who take Maimonides at his word—that the *Mishneh Torah* was in effect written to replace the Talmud—are right, then we certainly strengthen the claim that Maimonides understood the authority of the Rabbis in purely formal, not inherent terms. Otherwise, how could he allow himself the liberty of seeking to replace their work? On this whole issue, see Hannah Kasher, "Talmud Torah as a Means of Apprehending God in Maimonides' Teachings," *Jerusalem Studies in Jewish Thought* 5 (1986): 71–81 (Hebrew) and the sources cited there.

6.   Maimonides' discussion of the institution of the evening prayer may also be mentioned as confirming my claim that he viewed the authority of the Rabbis in formal, not inherent terms. See Blidstein, *Ha-Tefilah* . . . , pp. 49–52, esp. note 80.

7.   See above, chapter 5, section v.

8.   As Sh. Z. Havlin has pointed out, Maimonides often uses the term "all" (*kol*) in the sense of "most." See Havlin, "On 'Literary Sealing' . . . ," p. 151.

9.   Fred Rosner trans., *Maimonides' Commentary on the Mishnah, Tractate Sanhedrin* (New York: Sepher-Hermon Press, 1981), pp. 4–5. In Rav Kafih's edition, pp. 147–48.

10.   As we see in the text quoted just below.

11.   Which only the properly ordained may do.

12.   Recall that in his Introduction to the *Mishneh Torah* Maimonides grounds the authority of the Rabbis in part on the fact that they were segments of an unbroken chain of tradition stretching back to Moses. The texts here indicate that this criterion was less important to Maimonides than his first two (that the Talmud is the last halakhic text to enjoy the assent of all Israel and that it was promulgated by the Rabbis as a cohesive body).

Chapter 7: Concluding (Quasi-) Scientific Postscript

1.   The late Shlomo Pines may be cited as a distinguished example of this approach. For details, see Warren Zev Harvey, "Professor Shlomo Pines and his Approach to Jewish Thought," *Jerusalem Studies in Jewish Thought* 7 (1988) (=*Shlomo Pines Jubilee Volume*): 1–16 (Hebrew).

2.   See my "Maimonides on the Science of the *Mishneh Torah*—Provisional or Permanent," *AJSReview* 18 (1993): 169–94.

3. These points are discussed above in chapter 4.

4. On this, see Lawrence Kaplan, "*Daas Torah*: A Modern Conception of Rabbinic Authority," in Moshe Sokol ed., *Rabbinic Authority and Personal Autonomy* (Northvale, NJ: Jason Aronson, 1992): 1–60. For a polemical response to (a caricature of) Kaplan, see Berel Wein, "Daas Torah: An Ancient Definition of Authority and Responsibility in Jewish Life," *Jewish Observer* (October, 1994), pp. 4–9. Further on this subject, see the symposium on rabbinic authority in *Tradition* 27, no 4 (1993).

5. I owe this formulation to my friend David Novak.

References

Abramson, Shraga. "On the History of the Medieval Literary Debate on *Hagavei ha-Sela.*" *Sinai* 87 (1980): 25–33 (Hebrew).

Abravanel, Isaac. *Commentary on the Torah.* Jerusalem: Bnai Arbel, 1964.

Abravanel, Isaac. *"Me-ha-Abravanel le-Helek Shlishi me-ha-Moreh."*

Alpert, Pinhas. " 'Decline of the Generations' or Progress?!" *Gillayon* (Summer 1974), pp. 44–48 (Hebrew).

Altmann, Alexander. "Astrology," *Encyclopaedia Judaica.* vol 3. Jerusalem: Keter, 1971, cols. 788–95.

Arieli, Nahum. "Halevi's Conception of Halakhah." *Da'at* 1 (1978): 43–53 (Hebrew).

Baneth, David. "Maimonides' Philosophical Terminology." *Tarbiz* 6 (1935): 258–84 (Hebrew).

Berger, Michael Seth. "The Authority of the Babylonian Talmud: Analysis of its Justification and a Proposal for a Contemporary Model." Ph.D. Diss., Columbia University, 1992.

Berman, Lawrence V. "Review of Shlomo Pines' translation of the *Guide of the Perplexed.*" *Journal of the American Oriental Society* 85 (1965): 410–13.

Blech, Benjamin. "Learning from Heretics." *Tradition* 25 (1990): 12–17.

Blidstein, Gerald (Ya'akov). " 'Even if He Tells You Right is Left': The Validity of Moral Authority in the *Halakha* and its Limitations." In Moshe Beer ed., *Studies in Halakha and Jewish Thought Presented to Emmanuel Rackman.* Ramat Gan: Bar Ilan University Press, 1994: 221–41 (Hebrew).

Blidstein, Gerald (Ya'akov). *Ha-Tefillah be-Mishnato ha-Hilkhatit shel ha-Rambam.* Jerusalem: Mossad Bialik, 1994.

Blidstein, Gerald (Ya'akov). "Oral Law as Intitution in Maimonides." In Ira Robinson, *et al.* Eds. *The Thought of Moses Maimonides.* Lewiston: Edwin Mellen Press, 1990. *Studies in the History of Philosophy* 17: 167–82.

Blidstein, Gerald (Ya'akov). "The Concept of Oral Law in R. Scherira's Epistle." *Da'at* 4 (1980): 5–16 (Hebrew).

Blumenthal, David R. "Maimonides on Mind and Metaphoric Language." In D. R. Blumenthal ed. *Approaches to Judaism in Medieval Times* II. Chico: Scholars Press, 1985: 123–32.

Breuer, Mordecai. "Maharal of Prague's Dispute with the Christians—A New Look at *Sefer Be'er ha-Golah.*" *Tarbiz* 55 (1985): 253–60 (Hebrew).

Dessler, Elijah. *Mikhtav Me-Eliyahu.* Edited by Aryeh Carmel and Alter Halpern. Bnai Brak, 1965.

Dienstag, Jacob I. "Maimonides' Letter on Astrology to the Rabbis of Southern France." *Kiryat Sefer* 61 (1987): 147–58 (Hebrew).

Dinari, Yedidya A. *Hakhmei Ashkenaz be-Shilhei Yemi ha-Benayim.* Jerusalem: Mossad Bialik, 1984.

Drori, Zalman. Ed. *Sefer Kovetz Inyanim* (Bnai Brak, 1975).

Elbaum, Y. "On the Source of the Allegory of the Dwarf and the Giant and its Development." *Sinai* 77 (1975): 132 (Hebrew).

Elman, Yaakov. "R. Zadok Hakohen on the History of Halakha." *Tradition* 21.4 (1983): 1–26.

Faur, Jose. *Iyyunim ba-Mishneh Torah li-ha-Rambam.* Jerusalem: Mossad ha-Rav Kook, 1978.

Faur, Jose. "Monolingualism and Judaism." *Cardozo Law Review* 14 (1993): 1712–44.

Feldman, Seymour. "The End of the Universe in Medieval Jewish Philosophy." *AJS Review* 11 (1986): 53–77.

Fisch, Menachem. "*Qohelet* in Context—A Study of Wisdom as Constructive Skepticism." In I. C. Jarvie, and N. Laor eds. *The Enterprise of Critical Rationalism.* Boston: Kluwer. In press.

Fox, Marvin. "Nahmanides on the Status of Aggadot: Perspectives on the Disputation at Barcelona, 1263." *Journal of Jewish Studies* 40 (1989): 95–109.

Fox, Marvin. "Prayer in the Thought of Maimonides." In G. Cohen ed. *Ha-Tefilah ha-Yehudit: Hemshekh vi-Hiddush* (Ramat Gan: Bar Ilan University Press, 1978): 142–67 (Hebrew). English in: *Interpreting Maimonides* (Chicago: University of Chicago Press, 1990), pp. 297–321.

Frankel, Yonah. *Darko shel Rashi be-Ferusho le-Talmud ha-Bavli.* Jerusalem: Magnes, 1980.

Freschel, Tuvia. In *Ha-Doar*, 11 Iyyar 5734, p. 425, and 29 Tevet 5736, p. 136 (Hebrew).

Freschel, Tuvia. In *Sinai* 78 (1976), p. 288 (Hebrew).

Freudenthal, Gad. "Maimonides' Astrology in Context: Cosmology, Physics, Medicine, and Providence." In Fred Rosner, and Samuel Kottek eds. *Moses Maimonides: Physician, Scientist, and Philosopher.* Northvale, NJ: Jason Aronson, 1993: 77–90.

Fuss, Abraham M. "The Study of Science and Philosophy Justified by Jewish Tradition," *The Torah U-Madda Journal* 5 (1994): 101–14.

Goldfeld, Leah Naomi. "Laws of Kings, their Wars, and the King Messiah." *Sinai* 91 (1983): 67–79 (Hebrew).

Halkin, Abraham S., and David Hartman, *Crisis and Leadership.* Philadelphia: Jewish Publication Society, 1985.

Harris, Jay. *How Do We Know This? Midrash and the Fragmentation of Modern Judaism* (Albany: SUNY Press, 1995).

Harvey, Steven. "Did Maimonides' Letter to Samuel ibn Tibbon Determine Which Philosophers Would be Studied by Later Jewish Thinkers?" *Jewish Quarterly Review* 83 (1992): 51–70.

Harvey, Warren Zev. "How to Begin to Study the *Guide of the Perplexed* I.1." *Da'at* 21 (1988): 5–23 (Hebrew).

Harvey, Warren Zev. "Professor Shlomo Pines and his Approach to Jewish Thought." *Jerusalem Studies in Jewish Thought* 7 (1988) (=*Shlomo Pines Jubilee Volume*): 1–16 (Hebrew).

Havazelet, Meir. *Maimonides and the Gaonites.* Jerusalem/New York: Sura, 1967 (Hebrew).

Havlin, Shlomo Z. "Maimonides' *Mishneh Torah*—End of the Gaonic Period." *Ha-Ma'ayan* 5 (1965): 41–59 (Hebrew).

Havlin, Shlomo Z. "On 'Literary Sealing' as the Foundation for the Division of Halakhah into Epochs." In *Mehkarim be-Safrut ha-Talmudit.* Jerusalem: Israel Academy of Sciences, 1983: 148–92 (Hebrew).

Herzog, Isaac. *Judaism: Law and Ethics.* London: Soncino, 1974.

Hirsch, Samson Raphael. *The Nineteen Letters of Ben Uziel.* Translated by Bernard Drachman. New York: Funk and Wagnalls, 1899.

Hoenig, Sidney B. *The Great Sanhedrin.* Philadelphia: Dropsie College, 1953.

Ivry, Alfred. "Islamic and Greek Influences on Maimonides' Philosophy." S. Pines and Y. Yovel eds. *Maimonides and Philosophy.* Dordrecht: Martinus Nijhoff, 1986: 139–56.

Ivry, Alfred. "Philosophical Translations from the Arabic in Hebrew During the Middle Ages." In *Recontres de cultures dans la philosophie médiévale: traductions et traducteurs de l'antiquité tardive au xiv siècle.* Louvain-La-Neuve: Universite Catholique de Louvain, 1990: 167–86.

Jacobs, Louis. *Holy Living: Saints and Saintliness in Judaism.* Northvale, NJ: Jason Aronson, 1990.

Jacobs, Louis. *Theology in the Responsa.* London: Routledge and Kegan Paul, 1975.

Kanarfogel, Ephraim. "Compensation for the Study of Torah in Medieval Rabbinic Thought." Ruth Link-Salinger ed. *Of Scholars, Savants, and their Texts.* New York: Peter Lang, 1989: 135–48.

Kanarfogel, Ephraim. *Jewish Education and Society in the High Middle Ages.* Detroit: Wayne State University Press, 1992.

Kaplan, Lawrence. "*Daas Torah*: A Modern Conception of Rabbinic Authority." In Moshe Sokol ed. *Rabbinic Authority and Personal Autonomy.* Northvale, NJ: Jason Aronson, 1992: 1–60.

Karelitz, Abraham Isaiah. *Kovez Iggerot me'et Maran Ba'al Hazon Ish.* Edited by Sh. Greineman. Bnai Brak, 1990.

Kasher, Hannah. "Talmud Torah as a Means of Apprehending God in Maimonides' Teachings." Jerusalem Studies in Jewish Thought 5 (1986): 71–81 (Hebrew).

Kellner, Menachem. "A Suggestion Concerning Maimonides' 'Thirteen Principles' and the Status of Non-Jews in the Messianic Era." In Meir Ayali ed. *Tura—Oranim Studies in Jewish Thought: Simon Greenberg Jubilee Volume.* Tel Aviv: Ha-Kibbutz ha-Meuhad, 1986: 249–60 (Hebrew).

Kellner, Menachem. *Dogma in Medieval Jewish Thought.* Oxford: Oxford University Presss, 1986.

Kellner, Menachem. "Gersonides on the Song of Songs and the Nature of Science." *Journal of Jewish Thought and Philosophy* 4 (1994): 1–21.

Kellner, Menachem. *Maimonides on Human Perfection.* Atlanta: Scholars Press, 1990.

Kellner, Menachem. *Maimonides on Judaism and the Jewish People.* Albany: SUNY Press, 1991.

Kellner, Menachem. "Maimonides on the Science of the *Mishneh Torah*—Provisional or Permanent." *AJSReview* 18 (1993): 169–94.

Kellner, Menachem. "Messianic Postures in Israel Today." *Modern Judaism* 6 (1986): 197–209; reprinted in Marc Saperstein ed. *Essential Papers on Messianic Movements and Personalities in Jewish History.* New York: New York University Press, 1992: 504–18.

Kellner, Menachem. "On the Status of the Astronomy and Physics in Maimonides' *Mishneh Torah* and *Guide of the Perplexed*: A Chapter in the History of Science." *British Journal for the History of Science* 24 (1991): 453–63.

Kellner, Menachem. "On Universalism and Particularism in Judaism." *Da'at* (forthcoming).

Kellner, Menachem. "Revelation and Messianism: A Maimonidean Study." In Dan Cohn-Sherbok ed. *Torah and Revelation*. New York: Edwin Mellen Press, 1992: 117–33.

Kellner, Menachem. "The Conception of the Torah as a Deductive Science in Medieval Jewish Thought." *Revue des etudes juives* 146 (1987): 265–79.

Klein-Braslavi, Sara. "Solomon's 'Prophecy' in Maimonides' Writings." In M. Idel, *et al.* eds. *Minhah le-Sarah*. Jerusalem: Magnes, 1994: 57–81 (Hebrew).

Kreisel, Howard (Haim). "Maimonides' Approach to Astrology." *Proceedings of the Eleventh World Congress of Jewish Studies. Division C*, Vol. 2. Jerusalem: World Union of Jewish Studies, 1994, pp. 25–32 (Hebrew).

Kreisel, Howard. "Theories of Prophecy in Medieval Jewish Philosophy." Ph.D. Diss. Brandeis University, 1981.

Lamm, Norman. *Torah Umadda: The Encounter of Religious Learning and Worldly Knowledge in the Jewish Tradition*. Northale, NJ: Jason Aronson, 1990.

Landau, Yehezekl. *Ziyyun le-Nefesh Hayyah al Massekhet Pesahim*. Jerusalem, 1976.

Langermann, Y. Tzvi. "Maimonides' Repudiation of Astrology." *Maimonidean Studies* 2 (1991): 123–58.

Lauterbach, Jacob Z. *Mekilta de-Rabbi Ishamel*. Philadelphia: Jewish Publication Society, 1933.

Leiman, Shnayer Z. "Dwarfs on the Shoulders of Giants." *Tradition* 27 (1993): 90–94.

Levi, Yehudah. "The Sciences as the 'Maidservants of the Torah' in Maimonides' Writings." Fred Rosner and Samuel Kottek eds. *Moses Maimonides: Physician, Scientist, Philosopher*. Northvale: Jason Aronson, 1993: 97–104.

Levine, Hillel. "Dwarfs on the Shoulders of Giants—A Case Study in the Impact of Modernization on the Social Epistemology of Judaism." *Jewish Social Studies* 40 (1978): 63–72.

Lieberman, Simhah. "Introduction" to Menahem Recanati. *Ta'amei ha-Mizvot*. London, 1962.

Loewe, Judah ben Bezalel. *Be'er ha-Golah*. Tel Aviv: Pardes, 1967.

Luzzatto, Moses Hayyim. *Mesilat Yesharim: The Path of the Upright*. Ed. and trans. Mordecai M. Kaplan. Philadelphia: Jewish Publication Society, 1936.

Maimonides, Moses. *Guide of the Perplexed*. Translated by Shlomo Pines. Chcago: University of Chicago Press, 1963.

Maimonides, Moses. *Book of Commandments*. Translated by Charles B. Chavel. London: Soncino, 1967.

Maimonides, Moses. *Book of Knowledge*. Edited and translated by Moses Hyamson. New York: Feldheim, 1974.

Maimonides, Moses. *The Commentary to Mishnah Aboth*. Translated by Arthur David. New York: Bloch, 1968.

Maimonides, Moses. *Iggerot ha-Rambam*. Edited and translated by Y. Shailat. Jerusalem: Ma'aliyot, 1988.

Maimonides, Moses. *Medical Works*. Edited by Suessmann Muntner, Vol. 2: *Medical Aphorisms of Moses*. Jerusalem: Mossad ha-Rav Kook, 1959.

Maimonides, Moses. *Mishneh Torah, The Book of Adoration by Maimonides*. Translated by Moses Hyamson. Jerusalem: Boys Town Jerusalem Publishers, 1962.

Maimonides, Moses. "Letter on Astrology." Translated by Ralph Lerner in Lerner and Muhsin Mahdi eds. *Medieval Political Philosophy*. Ithaca: Cornell University Press, 1972, pp. 227–36.

Maimonides, Moses. *Mishnah im Perush Rabbenu Moshe ben Maimon*. Edited and translated by Rabbi J. Kafih. Jerusalem: Mossad ha-Rav Kook, 1963.

Maimonides, Moses. *Moses Maimonides' Commentary on the Mishnah—Introduction to the Mishnah and Tractate Berachoth*. Translated by Fred Rosner. New York: Feldheim, 1975.

Maimonides, Moses. *The Book of Adoration*. Translated by Moses Hyamson. Jerusalem: Boys Town Publishers, 1962.

Maimonides, Moses. *The Book of Judges*. Translated by A. M. Hershman. New Haven: Yale University Press, 1949.

Maimonides, Moses. *The Medical Aphorisms of Maimonides*. Translated and edited by Fred Rosner and Suessman Muntner. New York: Yeshiva University, 1971.

Maimonides, Moses. "Treatise on Resurrection" Translated by Abraham Halkin in *Crisis and Leadership: Epistles of Maimonides* (Philadelphia: Jewish Publication Society, 1985).

Malter, Henry. "Shem Tob ben Joseph Palquera II: His 'Treatise of the Dream'." *Jewish Quarterly Review* 1 (1910–11): 451–501.

Margareten, Yizhak Zvi. *Sefer Tokef ha-Talmud*. (Ofen, 1849; Brooklyn, 1983).

Marx, Alexander. "Texts By and About Maimonides." *Jewish Quarterly Review* 25 (1934–5): 374–81.

Melamed, Abraham. "Maimonides on Man's Political Character—Needs and Obligations." In Moshe Idel, *et al.* eds. *Minhah le-Sarah*. Jerusalem: Magnes, 1994: 292–333 (Hebrew).

Melamed, Abraham. "The Sources of the Image of the Locust and the Giant in R. Abraham ibn Ezra's Nedod ha-Sir Oni." *Jerusalem Studies in Hebrew Literature* 13 (1992): 95–102 (Hebrew).

Merton, Robert K. *On the Shoulders of Giants: A Shandean Postscript*. New York: Harcourt, Brace, and World, 1965.

Nehorai, Michael Zvi. "Maimonides on Miracles." *Shlomo Pines Jubilee Volume on the Occasion of his Eightieth Birthday, Part II* (=*Jerusalem Studies in Jewish Thought* 9). Jerusalem: Hebrew University, 1990: 1–18 (Hebrew).

Newman, J. *Semikhah [Ordination]: A Study of Its Origin, History, and Function in Rabbinic Literature.* Manchester: Manchester University Press, 1950.

Nieto, David. *Ha-Kuzari ha-Sheni, Matteh Dan.* Edited by Y. L. Maimon. Jerusalem: Mossad ha-Rav Kook, 1958.

Nisbet, Robert. *History of the Idea of Progress.* New York: Basic Books, 1980.

Nissim ben Reuben Gerondi. *Derashot.* Edited by Leon A. Feldman. Jerusalem: Shalem, 1973.

Peters, R. S. "Authority." *Aristotelian Society Supplement* 32 (1958): 207–24.

Pines, Shlomo. *Bein Mahshevet Yisrael le-Mahshevet he-Amim.* Jerusalem: Mossad Bialik, 1977.

Pines, Shlomo. "Translators's Introduction." In his translation of the *Guide of the Perplexed.* Chicago: University of Chicago Press, 1963.

Ravitzky, Aviezer. "The Secrets of the *Guide of the Perplexed*: Between the Thirteenth and Twentieth Centuries." In I. Twersky ed. *Studies in Maimonides.* Cambridge: Harvard University Press, 1990: 159–207.

Ravitzky, Aviezer. " 'To the Utmost of Human Capacity': Maimonides on the Days of the Messiah." Joel Kraemer ed. *Perspectives on Maimonides.* Oxford: Oxford University Press, 1991: 209–56.

Regev, Shaul. "The Vision of the Nobles of Israel in the Jewish Philosophy of the Middle Ages." *Jerusalem Studies in Jewish Thought.* 4 (1984/85): 281–302 (Hebrew).

Rosenberg, Shalom. "Emunat Hakhamim." Isadore Twersky and Bernard Septimus eds. *Jewish Thought in the Seventeenth Century.* Cambridge: Harvard University Press, 1987: 285–341.

Rosenberg, Shalom. "On Biblical Interpretation in the *Guide of the Perplexed.*" *Jerusalem Studies in Jewish Thought* 1 (1981): 85–157 (Hebrew).

Rosenberg, Shalom. *Torah u-Madda be-Hagut ha-Yehudit he-Hadashah.* Jerusalem: Ministry of Education and Culture, 1988.

Ross, Jacob J. "Maimonides and Progress—Maimonides' Concept of History," Yehezkel Cohen ed., *Hevrah vi-Historiah.* Jerusalem: Israel Ministry of Education and Culture, 1980: 529–42 (Hebrew).

Roth, N. "The 'Theft of Philosophy' by the Greeks from the Jews." *Classical Folia* 32 (1978): 53–67.

Ruderman, David. "Jewish Thought in Newtonian England: The Career and Writings of David Nieto." *PAAJR* 58 (1992): 193–219.

Safrai, Shmuel ed. *The Literature of the Sages*. Philadelphia: Fortress Press, 1987.

Saperstein, Marc. *Decoding the Rabbis*. Cambridge: Harvard University Press, 1980.

Sarton, George. "Maimonides: Philosopher and Physician." *Bulletin of the Cleveland Medical Library* 2 (1955): 3–22; Reprinted in Dorothy Stimson ed. *Sarton on the History of Science*. Cambridge: Harvard University Press, 1962: 78–101.

Scholem, Gershom. *Jewish Gnosticism, Merkabah Mysticism, and Talmudic Tradition*. New York: Jewish Theological Seminary, 1965.

Schwartz, Dov. "Rationalism and Conservatism: The Philosophy of R. Solomon ben Adreth's Circle." *Da'at* 32–33 (1994): 143–82 (Hebrew).

Schwarzfuchs, Simon-Raymond. "Les lois royales de Maimonide." *REJ* 111 (1951–52): 63–86.

Septimus, Bernard. *Hispano-Jewish Culture in Transition: The Career and Controversies of Ramah*. Cambridge: Harvard University Press, 1982.

Septimus, Bernard. " 'Open Rebuke and Concealed Love': Nahmanides and the Andalusian Tradition." In Isadore Twersky ed. *Rabbi Moses Nahmanides (Ramban): Explorations in His Religious and Literary Virtuosity*. Cambridge: Harvard University Press, 1983: 11–34.

Sherira Gaon. *Iggeret Rav Sherira Gaon*. Edited by B. M. Lewin. Haifa, 1921.

Sherira Gaon. *Iggeret Rav Sherira Gaon*. Translated (into Hebrew) by Nossin Dovid Rabinowich. Jerusalem: Vagshal, 1991.

Sherira Gaon. *The Iggeres of Rav Sherira Gaon*. Translated (into English) by Nossin Dovid Rabinowich. Jerusalem: Moznaim, 1988.

Sherwin, Byron L. *In Partnership with God: Contemporary Jewish Law and Ethics*. Syracuse: Syracuse University Press, 1990.

Stitskin, Leon D. ed., and trans. *Letters of Maimonides*. New York: Yeshiva University Press, 1977.

Strauss, Leo. "Progress or Return: The Contemporary Crisis in Western Civilization." *Modern Judaism* 1 (1981): 17–34.

Ta-Shema, Israel. " *'Hilkhita ki-Batrai'*—Historical Aspects of a Legal Maxim." *Annual of Hebrew Law* 6–7 (1979/80): 405–23 (Hebrew).

Touati, Charles. *La pensée philosophique et théologique de Gersonide*. Paris: Minuit, 1973.

Touati, Charles. "La problème de l'innerance prophétique dans la théologie juive du moyen age." *Revue l'Histoire des Religions* 174 (1968): 169–97.

Twersky, Isadore. *A Maimonides Reader*. New York: Behrman House, 1972.

Twersky, Isadore. "Did R. Abraham ibn Ezra Influence Maimonides?" In Isadore Twersky and Jay M. Harris eds. *Rabbi Abraham ibn Ezra: Studies in the Writings of a Twelfth-Century Jewish Polymath*. Cambridge: Harvard University Press, 1993: 21–48 (Hebrew).

Twersky, Isadore. *Introduction to the Mishneh Torah of Maimonides*. New Haven: Yale University Press, 1980.

Twersky, Isadore. "Maimonides on Eretz Yisrael: Halakhic, Philosophic and Historical Perspectives." In Joel Kraemer ed. *Perspectives on Maimonides: Philosophical and Historical Studies*. Oxford: Oxford University Press, 1991: 257–90.

Twersky, Isadore. "Some Non-Halakic Aspects of the *Mishneh Torah*." Alexander Altmann ed. *Jewish Medieval and Renaissance Studies*. Cambrdige: Harvard University Press, 1967: 95–118.

Twersky, Isadore. "The Mishneh Torah of Maimonides." *Proceedings of the Israel Academy of Sciences and Humanities* 5 (1976): 265–96.

Twersky, Isadore. "The Shulhan 'Aruk: Enduring Code of Jewish Law." *Judaism* 16 (1967): 141–58.

Urbach, Ephraim. "Halakhah and Prophecy." *Tarbiz* 19 (1947): 1–27 (Hebrew); Reprint in Urbach's *Me-Olamam shel Hakhamim*. Jerusalem: Magnes, 1988: 21–49.

Wein, Berel. "Daas Torah: An Ancient Definition of Authority and Responsibility in Jewish Life." *Jewish Observer* (October, 1994), pp. 4–9.

Wolfson, Elliot R. "By Way of Truth: Aspects of Nahmanides' Kabbalistic Hermeneutic." *AJSReview* 14 (1989): 103–78, pp. 153–78.

Wolfson, Harry Austryn. *Philo*. Cambridge: Harvard University Press, 1962.

Wolfson, Harry Austryn. "The Classification of Sciences in Mediaeval Jewish Philosophy." In his *Studies in the History and Philosophy of Religion* I. Cambridge: Harvard University Press, 1973: 493–545.

Yuval, Yisrael Ya'akov. "*Rishonim ve-Aharonim*. Antiqui et Moderni." *Zion* 54 (1992): 369–94 (Hebrew).

Zimmels, H. Z. "The Significance of the Statement 'We are not acquainted anymore' as Echoed in Rabbinic Literature." M. M. Kasher, N. Lamm, and L. Rosenfeld eds. *The Leo Jung Jubilee Volume*. New York: Jewish Center, 1962: 223–35.

Zimmermann, Albert. ed. *Antiqui und Moderni* (*=Miscellanea Mediaevalia* 9). Berlin: Walter de Gruyter, 1974.

Zlotnick, Dov. "On the Source of the Parable, 'The Dwarf and the Giant' and its Development." *Sinai* 77 (1975): 186–89 (Hebrew).

Zlotnick, Dov. "The Commentary of Rabbi Abraham Azulai to the Mishnah." *Proceedings of the American Academy for Jewish Research* 40 (1972): 147–68.

Citations from Maimonides' Works

General Index

Abraham ben ha-Rambam, 57
Abravanel, Isaac, 112, 113, 118
Abulafia, Meir, 114
Adler, Elhanan, 106
aggadah, 45, 106, 110, 114; and philosophy, 4
Akiva, 15
Alashkar, Moses, 22, 103
Alexander of Aphrodisias, 46, 106
allegory 64; Maimonides' use of, 114
ancients and moderns, ix, 97
antediluvians, 30
Aristotle, 33, 43, 76, 77, 91, 106, 118
astrology, 63, 64, 76,110, 112, 114,
astronomy, 77
authority, 97; essentialist vs. formalist definitions, 1–2

Babylonian Talmud, authority of, 85–87; redaction of, 85–86
Berger, Michael, 97, 102
Blidstein, Ya'akov, 102

chain of tradition, 121
Christianity and Christians, 74, 76, 104
courts, 40, 100; relative authority of, 79–81, 85–86
creation, 28, 31, 33

"decline of the generations," 3, 4, 7, 13, 17, 18, 35, 81, 87, 91, 92, 93, 98, 99, 103, 107; affirmed by the Talmud, 8–12; as historical reality, 37–54; explained historically,

54–59; medieval attitudes towards, 20–26; physical manifestations of, 106; rejected, 99; rejected by Talmud, 12–18; and non-Jews, 106; and hasidism, 98; as formal doctrine, 12
dogma, 114
"dwarves on the shoulders of giants," 25–26, 105

esotericism, 43, 98
eternity of the universe, 76
exile, 14
Ezra, 14

Faur, Jose, 118
Fisch, Menachem, 97

Galen, 77
Geonim, 86, 87, 99, 102, 115
Gersonides, 113
God, proofs for the existence of, 29

Habad, 92, 95
halakhah, periodization of, 8, 13
Halevi, Judah, 44, 118
Hazal, see Tannaim and Amoraim
Hillel, 13–14
Hirsch, Samson Raphael, 109–110
history, 81
holy spirit, 113
human freedom, 63
human progress, 69–81

Made in the USA
Coppell, TX
25 April 2021

54442126R00090